One Man Went to Mow

One Man Went to Mow

Robin Page

EXCELLENT PRESS

LUDLOW

First published in the UK by Excellent Press 2001

A copy of the British Library Cataloguing in Publication Data for this
title is available from the British Library.

ISBN 1 900318 15 6

Printed in the United Kingdom

Contents

Contents

Dedication

I am dedicating this book to Corset, that wonderful foxhound (criminal) who shared my house and life with me and who gave me so much happiness and anguish during the last twelve months.

This book is also for all those people with the 'country mind', in both town and country, who have supported the countryside through a time of crisis; all those people who marched, who demonstrated, who wrote letters, and who stood outside garages and fuel depots to show the world the huge injustices currently being heaped on Britain's traditional rural population by urban politicians, aided and abetted by their friends within the BBC. But above all this book is dedicated to all those farmers whose lives were ruined by foot and mouth and the millions of animals that were callously and needlessly slaughtered because of the closed minds, the ignorance and the sheer incompetence of our politicians, bureaucrats, Eurocrats and Euro fatcats.

Preface

————

In my last collection of writings, *Carry on Farming*, I warned that the countryside was in crisis. Many people did not believe me. This book shows the full extent of the tragedy overtaking the countryside, rural people and rural traditions. It covers an amazing two years; a period of time that turned my personal life upside down and saw me get the sack as presenter of 'One Man and His Dog', for daring to criticise my employers and for defending the countryside. It saw farming and wildlife devastated by the ignorance of urban MPs, who, with the same degree of ignorance attacked hunting and those rural communities where it continues to be a living culture and a vital part of community life.

For many farmers the nightmare of foot and mouth will turn out to be the tragic last straw. At the first debate on foot and mouth disease in the House of Commons, once the virus had struck, just thirteen New Labour MPs attended, showing both the government's and New Labour's depth of knowledge and their commitment to the countryside. Their reaction and attitudes were a disgrace and the Prime Minister, Tony Blair, was exposed as being one of the most shallow and manipulative of men ever to taken up residence in No. 10 Downing Street.

Normally I include a 'Countryman's Who's Who' in my books that mention politicians. Sadly on this occasion my contempt for those who rule us is so great that I do not want to risk transgressing the laws of libel. Of course I would not have broken the law knowingly, but our current laws seem to fall over backwards to defend the guilty, the dishonest and the devious, so I have decided not to risk it.

I would like to thank the Editors of *The Daily Telegraph, Horse and Hound* and *The Countryman* for allowing me to reproduce the articles appearing here, although on this occasion since my publisher is too old to worry about being sent to prison they are totally *unexpurgated*. I would like to thank too, Christine Puddifoot for typing the manuscript.

1

Sad Dog Days

I have never been without a dog before, but somehow it has not yet felt right to go out and get a replacement for Bramble. When a television or a piece of furniture comes to the end of its day it is possible to simply go out and get a replacement, with a dog it is different. A dog is not – or should not be – just a thing or a fashion accessory; Bramble was a real friend and an important part of my life and I miss him. I had him for virtually seventeen years, from a nervous, unsure puppy, to an old man with a character and mind of his own.

It is true that dogs are often like their owners and Bramble was a happy dog. He had a sunny disposition and I often think that most of my visitors came to see him, rather than me. But then for most of my life I have been happy too; it is only recently that I have started to become an angry, late-middle aged man, and that is because of the way in which the countryside is being treated by our dreadful politicians – of all Parties. Farming, country people and the countryside deserve better.

But who knows? Perhaps a dog will bring back some of the happiness, but what should I have? Bramble was the first lurcher I have ever owned and he was wonderful. He was a cross between a short haired traditional Norfolk lurcher from near Swaffham, and an Argentinean Bedlington terrier living in Lowestoft – what a mixture. The man who managed to secure such a union of looks and genes was the retired head-gamekeeper at Sandringham, Monty Christopher. Several years ago now I wrote a book called 'The Wildlife of the Royal Estates'. During the research Monty showed me the wildlife of Sandringham. Like many gamekeepers he was a good naturalist and he was also an expert on country lore and country dogs. He had always wanted to breed a lurcher that looked like a miniature deer hound, and with Bramble he succeeded totally.

So it is to Monty Christopher that I owe a huge debt; he gave me seventeen years of happiness. I had heard that lurchers made good 'one man dogs', but Bramble was more than that, he was a real character and a real friend. He went everywhere with me – except when he wanted to go somewhere else. That somewhere else nearly always involved a young lady dog from the other end of the village, or sometimes he just got bored with me typing away upstairs and so he would make his own way along the path to the farm to see what was going on there. At the farm he had a good friendship with the farm Labrador, Rinty, and then Jonah, and they would spend hours playing together and occasionally running off to hunt rabbits together.

Twice, as Bramble made his way to the farm, knowing exactly where he was and what he was doing, he was picked up by old ladies who assumed him to be lost. On the first occasion he was retrieved from an animal refuge, after a local boy had phoned me in panic: 'Robin, I have just seen an old lady steal your dog'. She had been a well-meaning but misguided old lady. On the second occasion we managed to stop a different old lady before she had driven off, aiming for the same animal shelter. On both occasions Bramble was not amused at his routine being so severely interrupted.

Finally, after a long and happy life the inevitable happened. I buried my old friend in the same beautiful little grass meadow that will one day house me. Tears rolled down my cheeks as I always get so attached to my dogs. Psychological experts tell us of course all about 'companion animals', but so what? I am an unashamed dog lover and I find nothing wrong at all in having a real friendship with a dog.

But the question remains; what dog should I have now and when should I have it? Many people expect me to have another lurcher, but I am not so sure. I do not think it would be fair on either the memory of Bramble or the new dog as comparisons would always be made.

Other people of course, expect me to have Border Collies, and the idea of having a Border Collie is quite appealing. The problem is that we have had them before and each one has come to a sad, or even tragic, end. Unfortunately the farm is near a road junction with both an A road and a busy B road running near it. Sadly, these days, drivers do not associate villages and farms with people and working dogs; they also fail to appreciate that speed limits are designed to protect the residents from travellers who do not know the area. Sadly most of our collies were hit by speeding cars and so we will not be having any more. Now I round my sheep up by banging the food bucket; under this system they will go anywhere with me.

I like Labradors too, and we have always had them at the farmhouse. They are big, pleasant dogs, but on a farm they need plenty of work. They make good cattle dogs and they also make excellent gun dogs, but we haven't really the work to keep a new young dog busy. In addition I don't shoot and in winter a farm Labrador needs to go with the gun. Usually when rough shooting, man and dog are in their element; I love eating wild pheasant, but I haven't got the time or inclination to shoot them myself and so I think a Labrador is currently out of the question.

Gordon Beningfield had a Border Terrier called Ted, and his widow Betty, still has him. He is a wonderful little dog, but he is quite wild and uncontrollable. My garden is full of wild birds and has been all summer. I have had more fledglings this year than ever before. I think a terrier like Ted would be terrible for my birds and so I must consider something else. Another friend had a Jack Russell. Again he is a dog of enormous character, but for ninety percent of his day he manages to become deaf. For the remaining ten percent he shows great difficulty in understanding the simplest of words such as 'stay', 'sit' and 'heel', and so I think all terriers are tarred with the same brush.

What else is there, Alsatians are too big. Dalmatians are too expensive; Greyhounds are too fast; Spaniels block the Hoover up during a moult and Poodles are not really my cup of tea. I do have a confession to make however. This summer I have been doing

3

some book research in the Cotswolds and while at Chipping Norton went to the Heythrop Hunt's Puppy Show. Oh dear, I think I have fallen in love with a foxhound puppy, but should I have one? Foxhounds are large, fit, bouncy dogs and what havoc would a foxhound cause to my living room bouncing about in there? If it got bored and made its way up to the farm, as Bramble did, how would it react to a little old lady stopping to rescue it? It would probably pick her up and carry her to the farm to join in the fun with Jonah. It seems to me that I have quite a bit more thinking to do before I come to a final decision.

2

A Suggestion for Digestion

Since the last chapter, the pace of life seems to have accelerated when I thought it was already going flat out. While my poor brother has been left finishing the drilling and the rolling, I have been travelling at breakneck speed from the very north of Scotland to the Southern tip of South Africa. In South Africa I had the good fortune to see whales – Southern Right Whales. They were given the name 'right' because they were the right whales to hunt. They were slow and so the old whaling boats, and even rowing boats could keep up with them. They made a spectacular sight, sixty five tons of blubber jumping almost clear of the water. The energy consumed must have been enormous, rather like John Prescott getting out of the bath.

Nearby was an island containing some forty thousand fur seals as well as a number of 'African Penguins'. The name 'African' is odd; last time I visited the Cape they were called 'Jackass' penguins, because the call they make resembles a braying donkey – a jackass. However, political correctness has struck

South Africa, just as it has in Great Blairland, and so the 'Jackass' has become the 'African'. Whether Africans make the same noise as the penguins is a politically incorrect question, and so I shall not ask it.

Unfortunately all is not well with these African penguins; various birds are stealing their eggs and in addition the odd fur seal is literally having a p p p p penguin. Then in turn, the occasional fur seal is being dined upon by a great white shark and presumably a variety of fishermen are trawling all sorts of fish remains through the water trying to get to the great white sharks. It is not the cuddly world of Rolf Harris, it is real life.

Sadly the story from Scotland is a similar tale of animal digestion, with the capercaillie, the curlew and the lapwing being the unfortunate birds being digested. Although in the world of Plastic Man, Tony Blair, all people and animals should live in harmony, nobody has managed to tell this to the wildlife. Consequently after hundreds of years of country people knowing that the fox eats ground nesting birds, the RSPB has decided not to protect their ground-nesting capercaillie at the spectacular Abernethy reserve, with the result that this year foxes and pine martens have had a feast; capercaillie has been enjoyed as starter, main course and sweet, and Abernethy is not quite as spectacular as it used to be. The RSPB, somewhat mortified at its simple lesson in predation, is blaming all the damage on the pine marten. This is a crafty, fox-like position to take, as of course the pine marten is protected and so the RSPB can wash its hands of all blame. But even so, I assume that many conservationists will not heed the warning as there are numerous schemes afoot to reintroduce the pine marten to an assortment of areas, conveniently forgetting why the pine marten became scarce in the first place – because it was a pest and killed both domestic and wild birds and animals.

Not only are great crocodile tears being cried for the Abernethy capercaillie, but they are also currently being cried for curlews and lapwing. Yes, it is true that sheep, rolling, draining and silage making have harmed the breeding success of both birds, but predation by crows, magpies, foxes, pine martens and sparrowhawks has also played a significant part, yet for the sake of conservational correctness numerous conservation bodies are just standing by and watching the curlew and the lapwing disappear before their very eyes. What is wanted is a simple ruling preventing farmers rolling grass after the middle of March together with a subsidy for those farmers prepared to leave silage making until after July 1st. Hand in hand with this should be a policy of predator control where curlews and lapwings are in decline and need protection, and that predator control should include sparrowhawks, controlled under licence. Sooner or later conservationists must learn that habitat management and population management (predator control – control, not extermination) should go hand in hand.

While in Scotland I heard a most remarkable tale. A *Telegraph* reader had written to a Member of the Scottish Parliament, the redoubtable Winifred Ewing. She may be redoubtable, but she is also evidently wildlife illiterate. The reader had written complaining of the proposed ban on hunting; Mrs. Ewing's reply was remarkable, it read; 'I acknowledge receipt of your letter dated 11th September. I will vote against 'ceremonious' fox hunting but I will allow farmers to kill the foxes when they take lambs' eyes'. Does this mean that this female David Attenborough of the Highlands cannot tell the difference between a fox and a crow, or that she simply doesn't know what she is talking about; perhaps the new Scottish Parliament should be renamed the Jackass Parliament.

3

Ten Years On

It seems impossible that it is already ten years ago since the murder of George Adamson. He died in a hail of bullets on Sunday

August 20th 1989, aged 83, at his beloved Kora game reserve, on the banks of the Tana river, in the Northern Frontier District of Kenya. Some people believe that he was unlucky and was shot by 'shifta', Somali bandits who were guilty of much of Kenya's poaching, others believe that he was cynically murdered as the Somalis wanted him out of the way; I tend to believe the latter theory.

He was a remarkable man, and he had a remarkable gift; he loved animals and he had an affinity with them. He was like a latter day conservation prophet, with long white hair and beard – Kenya's own version of St. Francis of Assisi, but a saint who liked to chuckle and see the sun set with a glass of White Horse whisky in his hand.

He came to fame through his wife, Joy Adamson, a gifted artist and writer who shot to international celebrity status with her book 'Born Free'. It was about the Adamson's relationship with a lioness, Elsa, and when the story was made into a film, fame and fortune were guaranteed – for Joy at any rate. That was one of the great ironies of the story. The good naturalist was George; the one who had the gift of looking after and communicating with animals; yet it was Joy who made the money and even at the time of his murder George had little spare cash. In real life Joy was a difficult, highly strung woman, and at the time of her murder in 1980 her first husband commented sourly, but honestly, 'All the world mourns Joy, except her three husbands'.

It was after 'Born Free' that I saw the documentary about Joy, George and their lions. She seemed pushy, shallow and conscious of the camera; he seemed quiet, philosophical and unassuming. It was also clear that he was the real naturalist and conservationist of the two. It was then that I decided that at some time in the future I must try to meet that old frontiersman – because that is what he was.

He had an astonishing life and sadly the wonderful world of high tech, Internet and Tony Blair will never see anything like it again. He was born in India, but on the retirement of his father, the family moved to Kenya and George's life in pioneer Kenya began. In his time he was a Government Locust officer, gold prospector, wild honey and beeswax trader, professional hunter and wildlife warden. He lived during an age when virtually every day brought its own story and adventure. He faced snakes, charging buffalo, floods, drought and daily danger. His was a wild Africa that would always be there and would always be teeming with wildlife.

But gradually things changed. The frontiers were pushed back; the wildlife was pushed back with them, and gradually it dawned on George Adamson that he was witnessing Africa in retreat; he had been lucky enough to see the bush and creation at its best but this fragile world was disappearing before his very eyes. I suppose if he had been a young Tony Blair he would have welcomed this change and described it as 'Africa preparing itself for the new Millennium'.

Fortunately, he was not a Tony Blair think-alike and he decided to dedicate his life to conservation and restoration, and that is what he was doing when I met him at Kora. He was trying to restore game and habitat to a reserve that had been poached and overgrazed, and he was succeeding. There too he had released lions and every day he would drive along the river bank checking for signs and contacting second and third generation lions born in the wild.

I was lucky enough to meet him eight or nine times in the 1980s. Just as George had taken a conscious decision to live for conservation, I had decided not to plan a normal career route, which gave me the freedom to meet people like George on a whim and a shoestring. To see him with his lions was remarkable. I still remember the first time, when suddenly Koretta appeared – a beautiful female lioness came from nowhere and immediately the look and bond of friendship were there.

They were still there when I met him for the last time five months before he died. He had three more orphaned cubs that he was going to rear for later release. He was a good man; his knowledge of the bush was inexhaustible and his motives were entirely selfless. It was at Kora too that I learnt much. In today's hunting debate we hear about fear and terror. I learnt that fear for me (so far) only takes place after an incident and that it results from my ability to rationalise and reason afterwards. When two wild lions walked past us at twenty yards, when we were on foot, and George had not seen them; it was not fear that came, but a huge adrenaline spurt. It was the same when the Land Rover broke down and we had to walk twelve miles in the midday sun to get help. Then, without George, or any weapons, we had to walk past a whole pride of wild lions, and again it was adrenaline that triumphed over fear.

When he died on that hot August day I cried. I had lost a friend and so had Africa and its wildlife. Almost as bad, I had a cousin who should have been doing research at the camp, but fortunately the call of the wild had come to his rescue. His girlfriend had arrived two days early and they had left for the coast.

The legacy of George Adamson is a determination in many people to fight for Africa's wildlife and its last wild places. It is a noble vision and dream. George was a good practical conservationist, but sadly part of his legacy has been clouded by 'animal rights'. Now, in the name of conservation, and even in the name of George Adamson, animals are returned to the wild, and Africans, some of whom have livelihoods threatened by elephant, buffalo and lion, are told that no wildlife must be killed.

But how did George Adamson reintroduce his lions? He shot antelope to feed them, and he taught them to hunt; he had to kill and they had to kill to get back into the wild. When there were no antelopes he bought camels from a nearby village and the lions dined on camel. If an 'animal rights' aura has been created around him and the mighty carnivores of Africa, what about the 'rights' of the impala, the lesser kudu, the waterbuck and the camel, shot as lion food. Didn't they have any rights? The greatest legacy of George Adamson is that he was a practical conservationist. He knew that conservation was not only about habitat management, it was about animal management too. It is a lesson that many conservationists and bunny-huggers would do well to learn today – and not just for Africa.

4

Plastic Man

Poor Mr. Blair, our friend 'bomber' is receiving a lot of flak from country people at the moment, but I would like to take the opportunity to thank him. Normally at the end of September I am the 'Home Made Wine Judge' at the Great Gransden Show, a traditional agricultural show in the south-west corner of Cambridgeshire. It is a very happy task in every respect, but this year I had to miss it as I needed to go to the Eskdale Show, in the south-west corner of the Lake District. My problem is that I am writing a book on all aspects of hunting, 'The Hunting Gene', and so I am having to rush around to some of the most spectacular parts of Britain, before Mr. One Nation Blair bans hunting. This, hypocritically, would turn his One Nation into Two; a hunting ban will be the final nail in the coffin for many isolated rural communities.

The odd thing about the book is that after writing twenty or so reasonably successful books I could not get a mainstream publisher to take this one on – political correctness rules. Consequently I am publishing it myself and if 'Bomber', 'One Nation' or even Herr Slobodan Blair bans hunting before the book is out, then all my life savings, and the financial contributions of several hundred other ordinary people will all disappear down the plughole.

Consequently, I had to make the dash to Eskdale. I have to say, given the choice of trip to the Royal Show, or even to the Millennium Dome, give me the Eskdale Show every time. Tucked into a field at the bottom of the Hardknott Pass and surrounded by mountains it must be one of the most beautiful Show grounds in the country. The Show stands for everything that New Labour does not; it stands for farming, tradition, rural communities and a living working countryside. There was hound trailing – hounds following an aniseed trail over the hillsides, with the first one back being the winner. The sport started when farmers with foxhounds on their farms for the summer would race one hound against another, but since then the trail hounds have been bred to be thinner and faster, as the competitive nature of the sport has grown larger and larger.

Then there was the foxhound show, where by an amazing coincidence, the local Eskdale and Ennerdale hounds won the major prizes. There was hill racing for those fitter and thinner than me and also Cumberland wrestling. Although hill farming is down on its knees there were dozens of Herdwick sheep too – in my view the most beautiful of all our native breed of sheep. Before the letters arrive I had better qualify that; according to Lakeland Myth, the ancestors of the Herdwick either came with the Vikings, and liked the Lakes, or they swam ashore from a sinking Spanish Galleon at the time of the Armada. The wool is wonderful and a couple from Yorkshire were making rugs, and yes, on impulse I bought one – I am not sorry. It was one of the best agricultural shows I have visited. As I left a *Daily Telegraph* reader approached: 'Please don't write about it', she said, 'we don't want it swamped with visitors' – sorry!

From Eskdale it was another rush – this time to Bournemouth and the Labour Party Conference. What a sad state of affairs it is when country people have to demonstrate for their basic civil liberties and a desire to survive. On Monday there was a protest by the NFU. By all accounts it went off like a damp squib; after the recent phoney hand-out by Gay-Wellies Brown the farming Establishment that runs the NFU wanted to pull out of the protest, but falling membership and grass-roots anger forced the leadership to march, quietly and half-heartedly.

The real voice and heart of the countryside came from the March of the Countryside Alliance the next day, with sixteen thousand people marching, representing the lost rural jobs if a ban on hunting goes ahead. The size of the March was not surprising, the real shock was the fact that hundreds of thousands of people had to be persuaded to stay at home, to limit the number to 16,000. By all accounts, it would have been possible to swamp Bournemouth with half a million people for the entire length of the Labour Party Conference.

To me it was amazing to see the delegates going into the Conference Hall. The hunting debate is a real case of men in suits with no roots, no culture and no wildlife, telling men without suits, but with roots, with culture, and with wildlife, how to run their lives. It seemed to me that the delegates were shocked too; they wanted to see a disorderly mob of 'toffs', what they saw was a cross section of ordinary country people behaving well and causing the police no problems.

The real problem it seems to me is Tony Blair, who does not understand the countryside or have any interest in it. One Nation to him means a bunch of shiny suited, homogenised, pasteurised, sanitised Euro-clones, just like him. In fact, he is described perfectly in the old Ray Davies song from The Kinks in 1969 – 'Plastic Man'.

Plastic people look the same. . . .
He's got a plastic wife who wears a plastic mac,
His children want to be plastic like their Dad.
He's got a phoney smile that makes you think he understands,
But no one gets the truth from Plastic Man.

I have challenged Plastic Man to a public debate on the Crisis in the Countryside – don't hold your breath.

5

Brussels Spouts

I am an unashamed hedgophile; I like looking at them, walking by them and sitting in them. I pick their fruit, burn their wood and smell their blossom. I plant them, cut them and when Badger

Walker arrives each year on his annual migration south, I help him to lay them. On our small farm, as far as I can make out, we have not lost a hedge in a hundred years; and if we have not lost a hedge in a hundred years, then it is probably safe to assume that we have not lost a hedge since the enclosures.

On Wednesday we are having a hedging demonstration on the farm, when Bomfords are using one of their posh mowers to show how well hedge cutting can be done with a machine if time is taken. Last week Badger arrived and we played in a hedge for two whole days, getting our skins scratched and our clothes torn, but thoroughly enjoying it and today the Countryside Restoration Trust is having a planting day, when we will be planting a new hedge. That hedge will be on the prairies we are transforming – 140 acres that over the years had virtually every one of its hedges ripped out, apart from an old parish boundary hedge that was too difficult to get at.

There will be an enthusiastic bunch of hedge planters arriving from all over the country. The record distance travelled so far was last year, from Peeblesshire, to Cambridgeshire, just to plant hedges; I can't see us beating that record for some time. There are other records to break however. On the last planting day, one of the planters bought a bottle with him of home-made 'wild plum gin'. It was a wonderful drink, one of the best I have tasted – like alcoholic plum juice. After two or three nips the world seems warm and wonderful and just thinking about it has reminded me that we ought to plant wild plums in the new hedgerow for this medicinal winter drink.

Over the last twelve months the hedges both old and new have served their modern purposes well. They have looked beautiful, they have helped keep the cattle in most of the time, they have provided many nesting sites for small and large birds, they have provided shelter during cold and windy weather, they have created real and important wildlife corridors and the fieldfares and redwings have enjoyed the winter harvest of berries.

But after saying all this, in farming terms, with this environmentally illiterate government in power and with ministers and a Prime Minister who could hardly recognise a tree in a wood, what is the point of worrying about hedges and working to create more of them? Under this indescribably ignorant government, those farmers who now encourage their hedgerows and who work hard for their wildlife are to be penalised. And what are Tony Blair, Nick Brown, Elliot Morley and Uncle John Two Jags and all doing about this? Absolutely nothing as usual.

The amazing fact is that the CRT's tenant farmer, Tim Scott, a farmer and conservationist of the highest order has had his subsidies cut as a penalty. A MAFF bureaucrat – Matt Oakey – Matt the crat, who describes himself as a 'Section Manager', has decided that Tim's hedgerows, sorry, his 'field boundaries' are too wide. So after years of people like me, the RSPB, the Farming and Wildlife Advisory Group and MAFF's own advisers telling farmers that they have been too harsh when cutting their hedges, MAFF now comes along, to penalise them for listening and taking action for wildlife. Field boundaries and hedgerows always were wide, until comparatively recently, now the madmen of MAFF are insisting that for full subsidies to be paid, no hedge or field boundary should be wider than two metres; what an insult, what an absurdity; what a form of measurement. The reason is simple; 'This follows further guidance from the European Commission about the full utilisation of fields according to customary agricultural practice'.

It is the unelected and unelectable (i.e. Neil Kinnock and Chris Patten) European Commission talking through its collective shirt again. Why, when there is still over-production does it want 'full utilisation', and to say that two metre hedges and field margins make up 'customary agricultural practice' is, in reality, customary European clap-trap. Two metre hedges hacked and battered might be 'customary agricultural practice', in Northern Germany, but it is neither customary nor traditional for most parts of the British countryside. We have some hedges nearer to ten yards wide than two, and what about those wonderful wide hedgerows that were once traditionally coppiced for wood. So how can MAFF officials actually write this stuff, knowing it to be nonsense?

Before New Labour came to power the repeated cry was 'we are going to reform the Common Agricultural Policy', and 'we are going to green farming with a flood of agri-environment schemes'. But what has in fact happened; the Common Agricultural Policy has reformed Labour, and of course with the Prime Minister there wasn't a great deal to reform. Rather than greening farming, Labour is industrialising farming still more – 'two metre hedges' is a perfect example of modern farming at its worst and modern farming damaging wildlife.

But the madness of MAFF exceeds even this. The reduction of farming subsidies for having proper hedges comes under the Area Aid Scheme. But some farmers also belong simultaneously to another scheme, the Countryside Stewardship Scheme, in which they are paid to increase the width of their field margins and hedgerows. This means to comply with Countryside Stewardship, they break the rules for Area Aid, and if they comply with Area Aid, they break the rules for Countryside Stewardship. Whichever way they do it, they could be in trouble with one or other set of bureaucrats and get penalised.

Farming is now part of a mad, mad bureaucratic world, barking mad rules are implemented by a Ministry that seems to dislike both wildlife and farmers; they in turn are run by politicians who do not care or understand and their strings are pulled by the unelected and unelectable in Brussels. I have come to the conclusion that there is only one course of action left to take – pull out of the Common Agricultural Policy as soon as possible – better still leave the EU completely.

6

It's Debatable

——

The debate held by the CRT at the Royal Geographical Society went exceptionally well, the speakers were excellent, the chairman was skilled and funny and the motion was carried by several hundred votes to one. Of course, as the audience was unashamedly partisan the result was not a shock, although in these days of control-freakism, I was rather irritated that one person considered that Countryside Restoration was a luxury, not a necessity.

It would have made excellent television and radio, but quite unsurprisingly the BBC's Countryfile, Farming Today and the Today programme were all conspicuous by their absence. I suppose it could have been that two of the panellists appear to be persona-non-grata with the BBC, and I wasn't even on the panel. Oliver Walston, barley baron, and it would appear, born-again environmentalist was at his witty and acerbic best. Yes, he can be irritating, yes, he can be bombastic, but he is knowledgeable, entertaining and he is a good broadcaster, but it would appear that he has been dropped by Radio 4. Without him trenchering away, 'On Your Farm' has almost become like 'Janet and John visits the Farm'. 'Oh, Farmer Giles, over there you have some animals, with four legs and a tail, that go 'Moo', what are they?' Fortunately the programme is now on so early in the morning that only insomniacs can listen to it.

Professor David Bellamy is another who appears to have disappeared from our screens, at least the BBC screen. Without a doubt he is our most hard working, effective and honest conservationist; perhaps that is the problem, he is too honest. He arrived at the debate after only having had two hours sleep in the previous twenty-four, and left early to rush off for another engagement in Dorchester. Again, his political incorrectness came out; he said that virtually the only farmland not in need of restoration was where hunting or shooting takes place. Then to compound his heresy, he went on to say that the greatest evil was intensive livestock production and transporting animals miles to slaughter. Such views of course appear to put him directly against some of the 'Bambi' and 'Freedom Food' policies of the RSPCA. It does seem that a very incestuous relationship is growing up between the RSPCA and the BBC; it would make a fascinating item for 'Watchdog'. Perhaps the great professor should start singing and dancing, become bland and talk in clichés, then he could become a presenter of one of the burgeoning pet programmes. It now seems that the BBC equates pets with countryside.

Fortunately another panellist was Barbara Young, ex-chairman of English Nature, and, I am touching my forelock as I write, vice-chairman of the BBC; so she could see these BBC rejects at work. She too was very good; although some people consider her to be a 'Blair-Babe'. Baroness Young of Old Scone, as she is in her new incarnation, has an independent mind and she certainly has turned English Nature into a more positive and active organisation.

I was expecting the debate to be David Bellamy and Barbara Young against Oliver Walston and Professor Sean Rickard, the former economic adviser to the NFU; but with the new eco-friendly Oliver, Rickard was very much on his own. The NFU was invited to take part but both the President, Ben Gill, and his deputy, Tony Pexton, amazingly found that their diaries were full on the night.

Sean Rickard came out with what two years ago was still the NFU mantra, that there were a third too many farmers and the economics of growing food should be no different from the economics of producing cars. There is a difference of course; if you make cars you don't have a responsibility for looking after otters, owls and orchids in your work place. For someone versed in the economics of farming and the CAP he also seemed unaware that it was the headage quota on cattle and sheep that had lead to over production by upland farmers, as well as the mishandling of the BSE crisis by successive governments.

Under the expert handling of the Chairman, Clive Anderson, the whole debate was entertaining, and the right side one. Before David Bellamy left he was congratulated by the Chairman on the quality of his 'dress T- shirt'. On the night, I was hoping to be smarter than David Bellamy for a change. Sadly, on a recent trip to the West Country I lost my only presentable jacket, so I failed again. If anybody finds a rather smart blazer with a skylark badge in a lapel – it's mine.

Having mentioned the BBC so much I suppose I should say that all the voice-overs have now been completed for the 'One

Man and His Dog – Christmas Special'. It has a very good slot: 6.00pm on December 27th, when shepherds throughout the country can sleep through it in a haze of sloe gin. It doesn't matter if they do sleep through it, just as long as they leave their televisions on, as viewing figures are apparently going to be a key factor in deciding whether or not the programme has a real future. The 'special' is certainly looking good and for once I was able to wear comfortable clothes and I did not have to dress up as a fat, middle-aged rustic male model.

Putting the voice-overs on was a completely new experience. We had been promoted from a converted garage in Watford – yes, that really is where the last series was finished – to the new BBC building at the White City. From the outside it has all the architectural elegance of a nuclear power station. From the inside it is remarkable; in the middle of this rectangular monstrosity is an attractive open garden. However, because it is surrounded by high walls and offices on all sides, nobody is allowed in the garden without wearing a hard hat, in case something is dropped from a window. This Health and Safety Regulation is wonderful, apart from the fact that no windows in the building can open and so nothing can drop out of them. In turn, this means that all the air in the offices is completely recycled, recycling colds and flu all day long – surely another case of investigation by 'Watchdog'.

Because of my lost jacket, when I arrived at reception I was firmly put in my place. 'What's your car number?' What did she mean? I travelled by train. The lady was impatient, as people wearing uniforms often are. 'Who've you come to pick up?' 'I've come for One Man and His Dog' I replied timidly. 'Oh, sorry' she smiled, at last, 'I thought you were a taxi driver'. I always knew I had natural charisma.

7

Postman Pat – or Eric

———

Every morning the postman, Eric, arrives at my door promptly between 7.15 and 7.20am. I am tempted to say *my* postman, but of course he belongs to the Royal Mail, or GPO or whatever it happens to be called at this particular time. Eric always smiles; he always has something to say, about the weather, the state of the world or whatever takes his fancy. He giggles too if he considers that he has said something profound. He talks, and giggles, with a broad Norfolk accent. He comes from the North Norfolk coast originally. I don't know how he came to be here in the first place, whether he came to work, or as a refugee; although I can't think why anybody would want to run away from Norfolk.

Every year he has two holidays away – in Norfolk – where he meets his old cronies. He goes wild-fowling and comes back with his accent suitably topped up. Because of his regularity I only need an alarm clock when he is away; then the replacements take hours to get along the lanes, roads and paths that Eric simply skips through. I suppose he has numerous short cuts unknown to the temporary postman from the town.

There was only one period of gossip regarding Eric, and that was all a big mistake. That was when a local farmer had a large Suffolk tup – nothing to do with Norfolk – also called Eric – whose reputation soon spread far and wide. His reputation was both for his appetite for members of the opposite sex and for his habit of putting his head down and charging at the unwary when he was out in his summer quarters. Consequently there were periods when people looked a bit suspiciously at Eric the postman; was he really a ladies' man, and did he also have a wild, violent streak. Certainly for a period people did not open their doors as wide to him as they had once done.

Soon however, the truth dawned, Eric's tarnished reputation was re-polished and the tup went to where all good tups eventually go – into a casserole. Fortunately all the other rams in the village have had more grandiose names and so Eric is again the favourite postman of everybody, without sin or blemish. Indeed when he recently skidded on gravel and nose-dived into the stones the concern was as great as if he had been nobility. Who knows too, with Mr. Blair's great egalitarian revolution underway, the Prime Minister could do far worse than ennoble Eric to sit in the Second Chamber of Government. He already speaks more sense than those who sit in the first. If he did become ennobled I wonder what he would call himself, 'Lord Eric of Registered Post'? Eric loves registered post; getting people out of bed early and smiling at them in their bedraggled states.

I have one big worry about Eric. It is an entirely selfish worry. What happens if Mr. Blair is right and everybody starts sending e-mails and playing with the Internet; do we get rid of Eric and settle for machines? Will the whole village, the whole country and the whole planet end up sitting in front of machines and communicating with machines – and this is what they call progress? Human contact will vanish – Eric will vanish and a service that goes back generations will simply disappear.

I believe that the village needs Eric, and virtually every other village in the country needs their Eric equivalent. The postman provides a touch of humanity, security and continuity. He knows everybody, he knows who should be doing what and so he acts almost as unofficial village warden. He knows who is late with their bills, who has got investments, who is doing good things and who could be behaving a great deal better. It also means that if Eric delivers a letter, somebody somewhere has actually sat down and thought about what they want to say and how they want to say it. They have got out a pen, paper and envelope; they have made a physical and mental effort to communicate; then the evidence of their activity drops through somebody's letterbox. With an e-mail it is different; it is just an electronic process.

Buttons are tapped and the impersonal message arrives on the screen of another machine. To make matters worse, all over the country there are now millions of machines, all left on, burning electricity so that e-mails can flow through quicker. This means that electricity production and use has climbed markedly and so the wonders of new technology could also be aiding and speeding global warming – a case of high tech creating no future – or the electronic highway leading to nowhere. Successive governments never have been very interested in global warming, it is their grandchildren that will have to deal with the problems, so who cares? That seems to be the prevailing attitude. The other thing about e-mails of course, is that you still have to answer them. The proponents of new technology keep praising instant communication; it is only instant if you have the time or the desire to sit in front of the computer all day and answer whatever has arrived. I haven't got a computer, only a word processor; I don't think I want anything else, as I would prefer Eric to call with letters every morning.

I have to declare an interest in all this, because I too have worked as a village postman. For several years I worked as part-time village postman in my village, and I thoroughly enjoyed it. I did not enjoy the postman's uniform, but I enjoyed the job. The clothes were terrible, they didn't fit and the trousers were so coarse that they pulled the hairs out of my legs as I pedalled. I suppose in today's climate I could have put in a huge claim for compensation. I still have several pairs of trousers. I now use them at harvest time for bale cart. The straw scratches so much that I don't feel my hairs disappearing, and making holes in the GPO trousers is a lot more sensible than wearing out better quality trousers.

I worked as postman simply because I needed the money to survive. As a youngish writer nobody wanted to read anything I wrote and so I had to subsidise my writing. It had huge advantages; getting up at dawn was enjoyable, as was getting up in winter darkness. Often it was a race, who would get to the post office first, me or an old fox that often used to be sitting outside, particularly on dustbin day. The dawn chorus was beautiful and always started before the commuter chorus, and the first violets of spring, or the first cuckoo, I always discovered from my postman's bike. Then if the weather was good and butterflies were on the wing I had time; work was done by mid-morning and I could go for a walk to see what was happening in the fields, along the brook and in the spinney. It was a time of happiness and learning. It was a time of fitness too as riding the bike six days a week was physically very good for me.

Now with some people wanting to read what I write the pedalling days are long past; it has its down side though – now when I hear a cuckoo or see my first orange tip butterfly of the year I have to go and write, instead of walk; I have to meet deadlines and talk to editors and try and check my appalling spelling.

There is another aspect I suppose. As I sit writing this chapter there is no danger of being attacked by an Alsatian or trapping my hand in a letterbox with a spring flap. Neither do I have to keep reaching down and stretching up, as no two letterboxes are alike. So, let's keep Eric, but perhaps he should also be paid danger money.

8

Glad Song – Sad Song

As I sit looking out of my study window I can see a wet, cold landscape. It is drizzling; it is cold and the cattle are standing huddled up in the lee of a hedge, out of the wind. Soon I have to go out into the clinging damp to feed the cattle and I am looking forward to it, as I am blissfully happy. It is part of that landscape out of my window that has made me happy, for not ten yards away is a song thrush preening itself in my forsythia bush. This is not just a chance sighting of a song thrush, I see one, two, three or even more every day, and I suspect that at least one pair raised a minimum of two broods during this summer.

Assuming that the thrush's main predators – cats, cars and sparrowhawks – took a number of the young, it still looks as if several survived and song thrush numbers are better than for years; why should it be? It is a question that has long puzzled me; if everything the conservationists and the RSPB say about habitat is correct, then we should always have had high song thrush numbers. The argument goes – it is loss of habitat that has depleted bird numbers – get the habitat right and the birds will come back. In the case of the song thrush it has not happened. We have always had good habitat on the farm and the area of thrush friendly land has been increased considerably by the work of the CRT next door, but still song thrush numbers have not been spectacular. It seemed that pesticide poisoning and sparrowhawks are other parts of the song thrush equation – but why have these wonderful songbirds come back now? We still have sparrowhawks and pesticides, and slug pellets continue to be used all around us. This is not a criticism, just a statement of fact. This year on the farm we tried to get away without using slug pellets on our winter wheat with absolutely disastrous results. Trying to farm in an environmentally friendly way can be costly both financially and emotionally when you get things wrong.

So, there must be a reason. Enter Chris Knights, farmer and film-maker extraordinary. For several years he has had a song thrush theory, and I think that he is right. On his 9000 rolling Norfolk acres he has some perfect song thrush habitat, yet some years he has them, and other years he has few. His theory is simple; he believes that in a damp summer, thrushes do well; rain and showers bring out the slugs and snails and as a result thrushes have plenty of food and they thrive. In a dry summer the slugs and snails stay at home and food becomes scarcer, making life harder for the adult birds and more difficult for them to feed their young.

This damp summer has seen two song thrush anvils in my garden, there are more down in the farmhouse garden and it looks as if our song thrushes flourished on a diet of snails – a preference they share with the French. Consequently I think the Chris Knights' theory is correct; one of the most important aspects of song thrush survival is rain; in dry summers they struggle, for lack of food, and in damp summers they do well because they eat well.

Although it seems to me that Chris Knights has hit the nail well and truly on the head, numerous scientists will claim that this is simple 'anecdotal evidence'. This is one of the very clever sides of science; when an ordinary person such as Chris Knights, or even me, sees a trend and comments on it, it is almost always disregarded as 'anecdotal evidence'. When a scientist hears or sees something and writes about it, it becomes 'science', and people pay large sums of money for it. Once money has been paid for it, then it becomes difficult to reject it and so sometimes reports that seem deeply flawed are accepted, defended and acted upon. One such report, it seems to me, is the now notorious Bateson Report on the red deer of Exmoor. When I read it for the first time I was flabbergasted at what was included as 'science'; I re-read it the other day and was even more mystified, not only by its conclusions, but also its methodology – a long word, included to impress scientists. At one point in the Report, deer hunting is compared with stalking. The deer hunting section is apparently based on analysis and 'scientific observations', some of which in my view is very peculiar. The information and conclusions relating to deer stalking come from a number of interviews with stalkers (anecdotal evidence) with no scientific tests or results whatsoever – if I am wrong, then please would the National Trust or Professor Bateson tell me?

At this point I had intended to write about the National Trust and the recent event which passed off as an election. Sadly I must write about the Third World nature of this election on another occasion as I have just heard of the death of a wonderful man who held the National Trust in total contempt – Raoul Millais. I had so hoped the old boy would reach his hundredth birthday, he was 98 and he had already invited me to the party. I called on him just the other week, to talk to him about hunting, the

24

Cotswolds and that nice Mr. Blair. He was instructive and amusing on all three. His eyes twinkled with mischief and he laughed as he gave a political analysis; but behind the laughter was a serious concern for the countryside and the country culture he loved. He mentioned the song thrush too, and how he believed the sparrowhawk was the guilty party.

Two or three years ago I interviewed him for *The Field*; it was a memorable interview full of wisdom, full of laughter and full of anecdotes and observations about wildlife. At the end of our conversation he said, 'I've enjoyed our talk Robin, take a picture, any one you like'. His paintings were on the floor, on the table, everywhere. I refused, but he insisted – the painting of red deer in the snow is now one of my most treasured possessions.

Listening to him was like experiencing living history. He travelled in Africa when it really was wild; Frederick Selous and Archibald Thorburn were his godfathers and he met Rudyard Kipling, Churchill and a whole host of artists, writers and politicians. He broke his neck hunting and received a telegram from The Queen on his ninetieth birthday congratulating him on reaching his century. With laughter in his eyes he told how he had written to her explaining that someone had got their maths wrong.

9

Winter's Way

———

In many ways this has been one of the strangest winters that I can remember. It started late, and in fact it hardly started at all. On our heavy land our cattle were out in the meadows until well into November; usually by the middle of October they are in the yards for the winter. Wet clay and cattle are not good winter companions and if they are not brought inside, the fields would turn into a sea of mud. By bringing them in so late it meant that we saved a month's straw and hay, which in turn saved a month of manual work, as we still use small bales which have to be carried and broken up around the yards. I suppose that is one of the advantages of global warming, that it will make our livestock farming easier; the disadvantages and the consequences from them, on the other hand, do not bear thinking about.

Since the cattle came in we have had rain and the grass has never stopped growing; there was even a stunted hogweed in flower in February. At no time either, have I felt cold. My longjohns have remained carefully folded in the cupboard and I have worn gloves about twice. Now I know I have a certain amount of natural insulation these days, but I actually like the cold and I have missed it. The saddest aspect of all is that there has been no skating; my speed skates are hanging up untouched and I have not ventured into the Fens once looking for ice. What with global warming, health and safety, and computer games, it seems to me that outdoor winter skating is doomed – another wonderful country tradition gone.

In my non-medical view too, it has been the lack of cold that has bred the 'flu epidemic. Warm weather always did bode ill; hence 'grass growing in January means a full churchyard'. In these parts there has almost been a queue to leave the planet. Fortunately my 'flu jab did the trick this year and I have had one of my most healthy winters ever – apart from my gently expanding natural insulation.

The other problem with the winter has undoubtedly been Tony Blair. The object of this chapter is not to be political, but I, like many other people welcomed his arrival in the top job in 1997. It felt like a good time for a change and Labour certainly talked about a good, happy, healthy, prosperous and environmentally friendly countryside when they were in opposition. Sadly once in power they have whistled a different tune – with the countryside in crisis, socially, economically and environmentally, Tony Blair can see 'no crisis'. The truth is that he does not want to see a crisis. Any informed view of farming and real rural communities will see a way of life and a culture facing extinction and all Blair can do is walk around grinning, saying 'there is no crisis'. Of course there is no crisis for him; I wish some of my farming friends and neighbours could have a wife earning £500 per hour, like Tony Blair; they would then have no crisis either.

It is odd. The only people doing well out of farming at the moment are those who run their farms intensively, like factories. Farming to them is simply a food production process – to grow their crops as cheaply as possible, and make as much profit as possible, regardless of the environmental consequences or what happens to the wildlife that once shared the land with them. On top of this there is also a new class of rural spiv – the farmer or landowner who joins the current get rich quick syndrome. With rural development out of control in Southern England, they sell their farmyards and meadows around them for development and in return they pocket cheques containing many noughts. In the last three years we have had five such offers for our farmyard near Cambridge; we have turned them all down. For me it would be like collecting thirty pieces of silver.

But amid the gloom and doom comes some very good news. On the land owned by The Countryside Restoration Trust, between the villages of Grantchester and Barton in Cambridgeshire, remarkable progress has been made and it is giving a message of hope for the future. If only the politicians would look, learn and listen. Two years ago, the CRT bought 140 acres of typical Cambridgeshire prairie, right next to the land it already owned. It bought it as part of its Sir Laurens van der Post Memorial Appeal, and called it Lark Rise Farm. For the first year it was still farmed in an intensive prairie-like way, but last year we changed the system.

The land came under two government funded 'agri-environment' schemes – the Countryside Stewardship Scheme and the Arable Stewardship Pilot Scheme. Under these arrangements, instead of simply getting subsidies for production, the CRT's grants and subsidies have been linked to the environmental work being undertaken on the land. With the enthusiastic help of the tenant farmer, Tim Scott, and numerous volunteers the wildlife dead land has been transformed. With grass margins, beetle banks, newly planted hedgerows and wildlife strips, birds, animals and insects have been given the habitat they need for survival and they like it.

In addition to this, the CRT now receives financial help for growing spring crops. This means that we can leave winter stubble and the birds and hares love that too. The other day I showed a journalist around the land and I was almost embarrassed by the amount of wildlife we saw – it was incredible – along the scrub by a ditch were at least thirty reed buntings and the stubble itself was alive with both skylarks and corn buntings. French partridges and pheasants were ten a penny and we saw at least three coveys of English partridges, one numbering twenty birds. To have seen so many English partridges on such a small area, in such a short space of time was remarkable and showed an astonishing shift of fortune for this wonderful symbol of a healthy countryside.

The CRT has numerous volunteer helpers and monitors. One of them is Bob Scott, once head of the RSPB's reserves management team. He is encouraged by what is happening and believes that already the CRT has the highest density of skylarks in Cambridgeshire.

But Lark Rise Farm represents even more – it is producing quality food and it is farming at a profit. Each year, the guru of agricultural economics, Professor John Nix, produces profit figures for farming according to market prices and costs. This year Tim Scott exceeded Nix's figures for three crops out of five. This was a remarkable achievement for it shows that if given the opportunity farmers could farm in an environmentally friendly way and they could survive financially if all the production subsidies were changed to environment subsidies. At Lark Rise Farm we have shown that wildlife can be brought back and our tenant farmer can make a living. There is a hitch however. At the moment only two per cent of farming subsidies go into agri-environmental schemes – this sadly brings us back to the plastic, smiling Tony Blair – it is time Phoney Tony put his money where his mouth is.

10

Winter Fodder

———

There are many reasons why I like winter; one of the most important is quite simple and can be summed up in one word – food. Yes, I like winter seasonal food and I like it best if it is British, with the odd South African orange or mandarin thrown in for good measure. If the mandarin is taken in liquid form as in Van Der Hum, South Africa's rather wonderful mandarin brandy, then so much the better; it complements sloe gin; it does not compete with it.

But just as I love winter food, I am totally baffled by all those people, now in a majority it seems, who go trooping off to the supermarkets in December, January and February to buy lettuce, asparagus, strawberries, peppers, tomatoes, cucumbers and fresh fruit salad, all out of season and all tasteless in comparison to their British equivalents grown in season.

But why should anybody want to eat fresh asparagus or fresh strawberries in the middle of winter anyway? Apart from demonstrating the unsustainable side of the 'global economy', what is wrong with good traditional British winter food? There are enough fine, tasty vegetables, meats, fruit and puddings to keep anybody happy and I can feel myself putting weight on just thinking about it. Steak and kidney pudding, meat pudding, Cornish pasty, stuffed marrow, roast pheasant, fish and chips, the list is endless and delicious.

Puddings too, have their own list of wonders; pancakes, currant roll, apple turnover, apple dumplings, apple crumble, spotty dick, jam roly poly, etc. etc. Oh dear, the mention of apple dumplings has reminded me that I have missed out dumplings in the main course list, and my hunger is increasing by the minute.

For any supermarket defender who is shocked at seeing apples in winter, claiming that they too are out of season – of course they are not, British Coxes and Bramleys are the best tasting and keeping dessert and cooking apples in the world.

By purchasing out of season food from the supermarkets, shoppers actually damage themselves in two ways. They deny themselves excellent traditional British food, and they also deny themselves the joy of seasonal eating. A winter of African, Israeli and Spanish asparagus and strawberries dilutes the pleasure of tasting the real thing when they are in season, in Britain. This, I hasten to add is not a racist or xenophobic view of food, but asparagus and strawberries are crops that do best in temperate climates and they do lose taste when grown in hot; dry conditions for the non-discerning sector of the British market.

British vegetables too, have a quality of their own, Brussels sprouts, cauliflowers, Savoys and that great edible herald of spring, purple sprouting broccoli – you can keep your mange tout and aubergines, in season or out. Of all the vegetables, I love Brussels sprouts best of all and if I ate them every day of winter I would not tire of them.

In the Autumn I had the good fortune to take part in the Cheltenham Literary Festival, to discuss with Duff Hart Davis and Ludovic Kennedy the work of that wonderful country writer, John Moore. What made the occasion even greater for me was the presence of John Moore's widow, Lucille, who actually sponsored the event.

Of all John Moore's many splendid country books my favourite is 'The Blue Fields'. His writing is funny, acerbic, lyrical and lucid and he sums up well the position of the Brussels sprout in our countryside and on our dinner plate. Describing winter he writes; 'at such a season the prospect which confronts you is gloomy in the extreme. Over the gate lies a black morass, in which yesterday's rain has made a chain of little lakes and upon which as like as not today's rain drips softly with a hissing sound rather like the noise made by an old and disillusioned ostler grooming a horse. The Brussels sprouts, melancholy of aspect, rise up out of the mud and are reflected in the dirty water;

their yellowing outer leaves, torn off by the winds or the sprout pickers, sail idly upon the brown lagoons. Of all the crops cultivated by man, sprouts make the dreariest landscape; and I believe the English are the only nation which spends its labours upon growing and tending them, which cherishes and takes pride in them, and which eventually eats them with relish. It is an addiction which we share with the caterpillars of the large white butterfly, and certain sorts of blight'.

My favourite winter meal is undoubtedly roast pheasant, with potatoes, Brussels sprouts, sausages, bread sauce and gravy. The gravy is important; pheasants are in fact 'free-range' fowl and some of the taste comes out during the cooking to allow delicious thick gravy to be made. This is in direct contrast to the supermarket broiler fowl; there the bird is so tasteless that various sauces and additives have to be sold to give it taste, rather than take it away. The other good thing about pheasant is that it is often as cheap as a broiler fowl, but it has had a much happier life.

Whenever we have game we always start the meal with 'light pudding'. It is a delicious start to the meal and it is an old recipe handed down from my mother, from her mother, from her mother before that. How far back it goes I do not know, but it is delicious and I have only ever seen it written down in my own books.

The ingredients are simple – 8 ounces of self-raising flour, 1 teaspoon of baking powder; 3 ounces of margarine, two eggs and a small quantity of milk. The margarine is rubbed into the flour, and then the beaten eggs stirred in. Milk should be added, but not too much; the mixture should be quite stiff and definitely not runny. It is then baked for twenty minutes, until it has risen and the top is crisp. In this quantity the pudding is large enough for between six and eight people. It is eaten with just gravy, and the same plates should then be used for the pheasant to save washing up. There should be lashings of gravy available, as we also once knew the pudding as 'blotting paper pudding'. It tastes far better cooked in imperial measurements than in metric, just as a pound of apples sounds and tastes better than a kilo.

11

Fouled Fowl

Unfortunately, this is a very depressing chapter. It started when I read a letter in the *Daily Telegraph* from Rachel Newman, the RSPCA's 'Head of Prosecutions'. I was stunned. For some reason, the RSPCA has a fixation on fox disembowelment. For this to happen, the dog or hound would have to catch the fox, turn it on its back, release its grip and bite the fox before being bitten itself. It is, of course, nonsense.

Several years ago, I had a pet vixen: she was killed, we assume by a dog. She was unmarked apart from puncture holes at the back of her neck. Similarly, Bramble and the old farm Labrador, Rinty, killed an elderly vixen one day. Rinty shook her like a rat. She died instantly and was virtually unmarked. So why does the RSPCA continue with its fixation on disembowelment?

In 1996, the RSPCA ran an advertisement featuring a disembowelled fox; omitting to say that the animal had been shot. As a consequence, it fell foul of the Advertising Standards Agency. In her letter Rachel Newman spoke of veterinary post-mortem reports confirming her claim. When I phoned to ask for the reports, I was told I could not have them – they were confidential.

What puzzles me is why the RSPCA does not do more to campaign against real animal abuse. Where are the full-page ads exposing the outrage of the closure of slaughterhouses and the great distances animals now have to travel from farm to abattoir?

For humanely killed, stress-free animals, slaughter needs to be as close to the farm as possible. Under the European directive, the reverse has happened: with unnecessary slaughterhouse closures, due to ridiculous hygiene regulations and unacceptable costs, animals are now being transported many miles to die.

32

The RSPCA has produced a charter for animal 'welfare standards', but this does not include a limit on the distances animals travel. It only gives a time limit of eight hours. This means that animals can be transported hundreds of miles and still be sold under the RSPCA's 'Freedom Food' label, a system set up to improve animal welfare. It is beyond my comprehension how a meat-monitoring system designed to protect animals can fail to take into account the suffering caused by long, gruelling journeys.

But there is worse to come: the killing of Britain's 800 million broiler fowl. Up to 60,000 can be dispatched a day in one slaughterhouse alone. The birds are shackled, hung upside down on a moving line and dunked into a water bath containing a submerged electrode. Some are stunned, some are killed and up to 2 percent – 1,200 birds – can remain conscious. The RSPCA's 'Welfare Standards for Chickens' states; 'birds that fail to be properly stunned must be humanely slaughtered before entering the scalding tank'. Strange, that: I thought killing by using the 'electrically live stunning bath' was supposed to be humane. So, with this method, some birds are 'humanely killed' twice.

The 'Welfare Standards' go on to say: 'The most reliable indicator that a bird is properly stunned by the low-voltage method is the electropletic fit. The characteristics of this condition are: neck arched with head directed vertically; open eyes; wings held close to the body; rigidly extended legs; and constant rapid body tremors. The physical conditions of the electropletic fit are shorter lasting and less profound when cardiac arrest is induced at stunning'.

Oh dear – there is more. The RSPCA instructions continue; 'Carotid arteries and jugular veins must be effectively severed using a ventral cut. This must be checked by the appointed member of staff, who must be given sufficient time to sever the blood vessels manually, if necessary. No more than 10 seconds must elapse between stunning and neck-cutting'. These birds are then sold as 'Freedom Food' approved by the organisation that finds fox hunting immoral.

12

Unemployed, Unemployable
But Happy

Doesn't time fly when you are enjoying yourself. December 31st, today, is a very important date for me. It is exactly thirty years ago that I was sacked from my last period of orthodox, gainful employment and I have had to live by my wits, or lack of them, ever since. In keeping with the victim/blame society in which we live, it was, of course, not my fault I was sacked. I blame my parents. When I asked my father if I could join him and my brother on the farm, his reply was simple and brief: 'No', he said, with no hint of variation or compromise. My mother was guilty too, she had a simple yet devastating philosophy of life: 'Say what you mean, tell the truth and don't hold grudges'. Sadly, few people in the big wide world seem to agree with her.

So, denied employment on the farm I sought employment away from the farm. I didn't last long at Nottingham Teachers Training College. I was there in the middle of all the trendy teaching nonsense of the early Sixties. I discovered that some of those in authority do not always like people saying what they mean; they don't always like the truth and they do hold grudges. As a result I found myself out of teachers training college, as well as the farm.

I decided to become a civil servant and went for an interview at Savile Row; for someone of my sartorial elegance that in itself was a huge shock to the system. If I couldn't farm I hoped I could get into the Ministry of Agriculture. That, in my early twenties, really showed my innocence. So, the Ministry of Agriculture was first on my list, the Forestry Commission was second, and the

National Assistance Board (now Social Security) was bottom of the list at about number twenty. I sailed through the interview with ease and became an Executive Officer with the National Assistance Board. The policy seemed to be that civil servants should have no knowledge of the department they go into and they should not be interested in it either – judging from some of the civil servants I have met in recent years it is a policy that could still be in place.

On becoming a Special Investigator I discovered a situation that is still tormenting the politicians today. Millions of pounds were being spent on the work-shy and feckless and social security applications were seen by some as a sort of bingo. Sometimes they were lucky, sometimes they were not. People were applying as unemployed when still at work; desperate women claimed to have been deserted when they were still locked into a loving, or lusting relationship and so it went on. In addition those on strike were receiving state benefits to stay on strike; the whole system was a fiasco. To cap it all, the Minister, Richard Crossman, and his sidekick David Ennals frequently appeared on television to say what a good system they were running.

'They can't say that, that's totally dishonest', I told my superiors, with an innocence that today I find hard to believe. 'They can', they replied, 'they are politicians'. So, after being duly shocked I wrote an article in the hope of anonymous publication and sent it to *The Spectator*. The phone went and I was summoned to London again by the editor; he was a chubby, jovial man with curly hair. Since then he has written a slimmer's cook book, as a result he is now a thin, jovial man with curly hair, but through some quirk of nature he still seems to have the same amount of skin as when he was chubby. I think I will give Nigel Lawson's cookbook a miss.

The anonymous article appeared, followed by several more. Crossman and Ennals were outraged, and in the course of time my identity was discovered and I was sacked, for telling the truth. Messrs. Crossman and Ennals were ennobled for playing the party political game and telling whoppers. My last day of paid employment was 31/12/1969. So my mother's philosophy had been a great success; at the age of twenty-six, young, keen and innocent, it had got me the sack and I was unemployed – since then I have become unemployable. For good measure government heavies even visited me at home and threatened me with prosecution under the Official Secrets Act if I wrote again. So giving my mother's philosophy a second go, I wrote some articles in the *Daily Telegraph* and the heavies crawled back under their stones.

Until then I had always assumed that writing books and articles required an Oxbridge degree and connections. But as a Cambridgeshire peasant I decided to give the pen, and self-employment, a go. Thirty years on I am still doing it, although my brother now also occasionally lets me wield a muck fork or drive the tractor as well.

One current MP outraged by my behaviour at the time was Frank Field, then Director of the Child Poverty Action Group. Two years ago when he appeared to be concerned at abuse in the Social Security system I wrote congratulating him on his change of view, although I added that I was sorry it had taken him twenty-eight years. Strange to say I did not receive a reply. Sadly it seems that many MP's have had sense of humour by-pass operations.

Now thirty years later it is time for another battle; what a way to start the year 2000, I think as a non-hunter, my interest in hunting is again based on my old mother's philosophy; so many of those opposed to hunting do not say what they mean; they do not tell the truth and they do hold grudges. Consequently I still dislike falsehoods and manipulation today, just as much as I did when I was twenty-six. What has spurred me on to write a book on hunting, is that after twenty-three successful books, I could not find a mainstream publisher willing to take on a politically incorrect subject. 'The Hunting Gene' was also turned down by BBC television and Channel 4. Some would say 'quite right, editorial decisions'. I would say 'censorship and political correctness'. So I have just completed the book, and with invaluable help from some of the best photographers and artists in the country, I am going to publish it myself, and submit it as evidence to the inquiry into hunting under Lord Burns.

Thirty years ago I got the sack and lost a career over principle; it was worth it. Thirty years on I am risking my shirt and my roof for free speech and openness again; it is also worth it. It makes for an interesting life and it seems to me that it is certainly more fulfilling and honest than being a civil servant or a politician.

13

Swan-Upping

I do not want to shock too many people of a fragile disposition, but I've been hunting again; it was a very exciting hunt and we caught our quarry. The drama started when my neighbour turned fifty. If he had a full head of hair he would look about thirty, but sadly most of his follicles migrated years ago. For this great milestone in his life, his wife bought him two beautiful black swans for their lake. The black swan is a magnificent bird and they looked perfectly in place bobbing about on their new home. They were young birds in full plumage; it really is a good thing that birds don't go bald as they get older.

I am not a conservation purist and so the thought of black swans on the lake does not fill me with horror and of course I have plenty of alien pheasants that come almost up to my back door to feed on most days. I have seen wild black swans in the Falklands and so it is quite good to have these birds just down the road.

They have not been welcomed by everybody however, and when two white mute swans flew in, trouble started. The aim of this story is not to tell a New Labour race parable – simply to state what happened. The white swans decided they did not like the black swans and soon the black swans decided to leave, so they waddled off over a field.

At this stage the story takes a very tragic twist. As the swans waddled along after dark they met Mr. Fox. Now this was not the kind Mr. Fox mentioned in numerous interviews by anti-hunters on Boxing Day; their Mr. Fox is so gentle and fragile that it cannot and would not kill new born lambs or take domestic hens; it spends its time eating cucumber sandwiches with crusts cut off and reading extracts from *The Diary of an Edwardian Lady*. Sadly on this day, our Cambridgeshire fox acted entirely out of character; despite being considerably larger than a new born lamb one of the swans became Reynard's supper, while the other waddled at an even greater speed to the nearby brook.

There, with the volume of water high and the current strong, the black swan lived safely and contentedly for several days. When I first saw him I could not believe my eyes; a black swan on the brook – I checked the level of sloe gin in my hip flask. For a bird so big it managed to hide among the reeds and fallen willows perfectly, tucking itself close into the bank and staying absolutely still.

The swanless birthday boy was happy that half his flock had been found – well, the other half had been found too, minus its head. A cunning plan was devised; four of us would go on a swan hunt. Bill was so determined to get his birthday present back that he wore chest waders. Immediately the search started, I was struck by a piece of inspiration that has so far evaded the world's greatest scientists – Darwin, Huxley, Patrick Bateson – it was possible to see that baldness could be an evolutionary hunting aid, for with the sun shining brightly, Bill's reflective pate could be followed through the thickest undergrowth. Similarly I thought, if he falls into the water it would also help us to follow his underwater passage.

We found the swan, which immediately tucked itself into a fallen willow. As two fat men, one bald man and a boy crept clumsily and noisily forward, with the hunting expertise of a rhino in a greenhouse, the swan was off. I was flabbergasted. With a strong current and expert navigation the bird was two meanders away before we had time to say: 'Missed it'.

We regrouped. Alan, the other fat man, and Sam hurried downstream, missing out many meanders, to string a long rabbit net across the brook. Then Bill walked one side of the brook towards them, and I was on the other, making sure not to fall in. If I had, then the remnants of my Christmas glut of mince pies, Christmas pudding and turkey would have sent a tidal wave speeding three miles down to the Cam, reminiscent of the Severn bore.

By a bend we found the swan again. I ran in front of it where the water narrowed. I missed it once more and not even my wheezing slowed it down. So we decided to drive it straight into the net. As the bird came closer Bill carefully went into the water to make sure that the swan did not turn back; the water was just two inches from the top of his waders. The brook narrowed, the current increased and the swan raced into the net. In a cloud of foam and spray Alan jumped on it; it looked like a scene from an ancient Anglo-Saxon hunting expedition. Bill was so excited that he slipped and the icy water filled his waders. Now chest waders have two main features; if you stay in your depth and don't fall the water can't get in. If you get out of your depth or fall over, the water can't get out; Bill was now encased in fresh, near freezing water

Alan and the swan struggled to the bank; Sam went for a vehicle and Bill squelched to check up on the wellbeing of his fiftieth birthday present. As he did so his colour went from pale to white. As we stood congratulating ourselves in the achievement the swan opened his beak and hissed. As it did so Bill's lower mandible dropped and he made a clattering noise, almost in answer to the swan. The black swan was loaded up and the three hunters made off; Bill was by now a quaint shade of ice blue. If he did not hurry to get a hot water bottle it seemed to me that he could end up being almost the same colour as the swan and speaking the same language.

Fortunately there was no Professor Bateson lurking in the reeds ready to take blood samples from the swan, or Bill, and I am happy to report that neither slunk away to die, or become traumatised. To round things off nicely there was also a happy ending. By a complete coincidence the next day I went to see my old friend Bill Makins in Norfolk, who runs the Pensthorpe Waterfowl Park, near Fakenham, which in my view houses the best wildfowl collection, in the most natural surroundings in Britain. After yet more mince pies and Christmas pudding, he announced that he had a spare, nubile black swan. She was caught, put in a box and now two black swans are swimming happily on my neighbour's lake. White swans are not welcome and we are thinking of a novel new approach for the rural fox problem. We will reverse what townspeople and urban local authorities do; we will start cage-trapping foxes, to release in towns!

14

Travelling On

Over recent years I have considered it to be a privilege to have been asked to speak to Royalty, nobility and peasantry. I have spoken to small exclusive groups and I had the astonishing experience of ranting and raving to 125,000 people in Hyde Park at the 1997 Countryside Rally. Last year too I regarded it as very special to be asked to regale thousands of country people at rallies in Bournemouth, Norwich and Cardiff. But despite all this, two weeks ago I received what to me was the greatest honour of them all, I was asked to speak at the funeral of our local Romany gypsy – Gypsy Jim Loveridge had moved on to another land, a land I hope he finds free of cars, harassment and overcrowding.

It was an honour for many reasons to speak at the funeral. Not being a member of Gypsy Jim's family, not being a Romany, nor a traveller, it was a privilege to talk about a real character; a real gypsy and a real countryman. These days traditional gypsies and country people have far more in common than many people realise; times are changing; the countryside is not understood and both the gypsy and the countryman are part of two endangered species in Blair's new sanitised and homogenised Britain.

As I stood at the front of the church it was moving to see those old Romany faces, still distinctive and immediately recognisable after generations of wandering the highways and byways of Britain. Most years I see them at the Appleby Horse Fair; but here they were; gypsy relatives mourning almost the last traditional wanderer of the tribe. His grown up children were there, my mother had taught most of them at the village school when the old horse drawn caravans came in and camps were set up in the driftways. She loved teaching them, 'They've got such lovely curly hair and they are so clean and polite'. Then as cars and lorries made the travelling life a nightmare, Jim and his family found a permanent campsite just down the road, where a friendly landowner and an enlightened council allowed them to settle down permanently.

Gradually the children married and moved away. One of the sons has just moved into a house for the first time. He doesn't like it; he can no longer hear the wind in the trees or the raindrops on the roof – the great separation from nature has begun. The service was moving. The family have few social graces; ties are rarely worn, hymns and the Lord's Prayer are difficult to learn when your clan is outside normal society – yet there was a real sense of loss, dignity, grief and hope.

Gypsy Jim was no saint in conventional terms; in the days of horses and mobility, a couple of lurchers always trotted behind the traditional caravan (vardo) and whenever Jim was around the local hare population plummeted. When I walked down the road for the first time with Bramble, my little lurcher, Jim almost fell off his bike in admiration. He screeched to a halt and offered me £25 in cash; he was disappointed when I turned him down and he told me I would never get a better offer.

His voice had a gentle, soothing tone especially when he talked about traditional ways. He made me a clothes peg out of a piece of willow and a strip of tin from a can which I still have. He insisted that when gypsies were free to roam there was never any need to steal and deal as new customers for pegs and lace and scissor sharpening could be found in each fresh area. It was only when travelling slowed and stopped that new initiatives had to be taken to try and ensure a regular income. Occasionally those new initiatives might be based on 'borrowing', which could be interpreted as having light fingers, but who could begrudge him the odd battery, bike or garden fork.

One day he asked if he could put his horses in one of our small meadows for a few weeks. We agreed that he could for £15; he kept them there for the whole summer and half the autumn too, removing them in the dead of night and we never saw our fifteen pounds. When he went to the pub his tally of pints could be estimated from the angle of his cap and when he was seen crawling along the road, it was best to help him up and guide him home. His gypsy remedy for drunkenness was simple, 'go home and have a long sleep'.

Some of his other cures were quite exotic from honey for boils to 'cowshit' for bald-headed women. It must work as there are very few bald-headed women in this neck of the woods. Ground ivy boiled in lard would, he claimed, cure eczema in men and dogs, and whooping cough was best treated with 'Robins Pillow's' (Robin's pincushions) boiled in sugar.

He was an expert horseman and in his younger days had visited many traditional horse fairs; 'you make a three year old horse a four year old by knocking some of its teeth out with a bit of metal like a chisel. It's not cheating really, 'cause it will be four next year so no harm's done'.

He was a regular part of the village scene for many years and he will be missed; his skills, his tales and his memories will never be repeated and soon his way of life will be seen as part of history. His was a happy life and with his passing another piece of the traditional rural jigsaw has been lost.

After the short, simple service a cavalcade of cars and vans accompanied the hearse along the main road to St. Neots. In death, Gypsy Jim found travel far simpler than in the days of his horse and vardo. Police outriders blocked off roads to ensure a safe and continuous journey – Jim with a police escort and no thought of tax discs and bald tyres. At St. Neots the coffin and the flowers were loaded onto a gypsy cart, with some of the wreaths in the shape of horse shoes. A pony then pulled him to his last resting place, with a procession of gypsies and travellers, most of them no longer travelling, following quietly behind on foot.

Soon it was earth to earth, ashes to ashes and dust to dust. His family slowly and carefully lowered a miniature vardo onto the coffin. Travelling was finished; a way of life completed; the last traditional gypsy of the village has moved on.

15

Foaming About Roaming

If I have understood all the triumphalist ramblings of the ramblers properly, then I am unique. Apparently I am the only person in Britain who has rambled over moor, mountain and meadow without being accosted by manic landowners waving shotguns. As a result, to allow greater access the government has come up with a 'Right to Roam' over millions of acres of moorland. By doing so 'New Labour' has shown that it is no such thing; its attitudes on countryside issues remain firmly entrenched in Old Labour, and the 'Right to Roam' is yet one more attack on the beleaguered rural community.

If the government really did understand the countryside then the place for any 'Right to Roam' to be granted should be on the thousands of acres of industrialised farming in lowland Britain. There, the policies of the CAP have allowed so much environmental damage to be done in the name of 'efficient farming', that it does not matter where people walk, or what they do.

Moorland on the other hand remains one of Britain's most fragile and endangered habitats. It is the final refuge for some of our diminishing ground nesting birds such as the golden plover, lapwing, curlew, dunlin, merlin and black grouse; the last thing that they need is a right to roam. What is wanted is controlled, responsible access that allows interested visitors onto some of our most attractive areas without doing damage. The right to roam will allow the exact opposite – damage, disturbance and intrusion, all for the political anti land-ownership baggage of the nineteen-twenties.

Sadly the problem of access is made more difficult by the way in which Britain has become urbanised, and so many visitors do not realise the damage they can cause. Over recent years on the farm we have had electric fences flattened and barbed wire cut, simply to allow selfish walkers and mountain-bikers to go where they like, regardless of the welfare of our cattle and sheep. Two years ago a gentleman with two buckets and two spades was digging up wildflowers, while last March I even caught somebody chasing my pregnant ewes. To make matters worse she was a vet student, (from London) who was trying to round up my sheep in One Man and His Dog fashion, with an old collie and labrador, neither of which had ever been trained. It was one of the most stupid things I have ever witnessed – yet if any of my old girls had aborted, who would have given me compensation – the Right to Roam government?

That is one more problem; if people not used to the hazards of the countryside are exposed to deep rivers, the sharpness of brambles, dead branches that fall from trees etc., who is going to be legally liable for any accidents that will occur? Does that mean too that the countryside will have to be tidied up to make it safe – if so wildlife will again be the loser. The government is good at talking eco and wildlife friendly policies yet in all its decisions connected with farming, the countryside and access it seems unable to grasp even the most basic facts.

Last week I took part in a debate with Marion Shoard at the famous Heffers bookshop in Cambridge; it coincided with the publication of the book 'A Right to Roam'. Although from her writing Marion Shoard fills her pen with vinegar, in fact she is a pleasant and amiable person. Oddly she supports the argument for a Right to Roam by comparing Britain with Sweden. What she fails to say is that in Sweden the population density is 19 people per square kilometre – in Britain it is 354. She also dismisses visitor horror stories as 'anecdotal evidence' – whereas her conclusions are based on 'science'. Surely the only difference between anecdotal evidence and science is that one is written down and one is not. From the audience reaction to the debate it seemed that Marion Shoard was quite taken aback at the strength of feeling against the 'Right to Roam', not by landowners, but from ordinary people worried about the effect of ignorant feet on our disappearing wildlife.

Although against a general right to roam, I am all for increasing access into the countryside. That is why on the Countryside Restoration Trust's land we are anxious to increase access. Unfortunately however, we are being actively hindered by the bureaucrats who administer the Countryside Stewardship Scheme. Recently I had a letter from a Mr. Braine, dated 9th March, telling me that all access arrangements must be ready by February 28th or else the CRT could suffer a financial penalty. Landowners are not allowed to claim money after deadline dates, but apparently bureaucrats can give deadline dates after they have already expired. The land in question should have a number of grass tracks almost ready for a permissive footpath. This is the same land that when the weather was ideal for sowing grass seed in mid-September, the Ministry would not let us sow until it had signed our agreement in October. By then the weather had turned wet and cold, the grass did not grow and so access is not yet possible. So thanks to MAFF we have no grass, no access and so we will be financially penalised because of the non-comprehending, inflexible

45

bureaucracy; this is hardly the way to encourage other landowners to copy our example.

16

National Distrust

I am beginning to think that I should see a doctor to check my genes, or else get somebody to check my drinking water to ascertain whether I am being affected by any chemical compounds seeping in. The trouble is this; most people when they come across a problem or see a challenge, go shopping at Tesco's or sit down to watch the television and forget their cause or concern.

Sadly my automatic pilot is different, and if I come across something obviously wrong I try to do something about it – hence this book, the CRT, the campaign to restore One Man and His Dog, standing for Parliament with the Referendum Party etc. I seem to have an inborn desire to tilt at windmills and the bigger the windmill, or windbag, the better. As a direct consequence my garden is overgrown, my car is dirty, there are ancient piles of letters that I do not have time to answer, and I have lost my Hoover – at least part of it – all because I am too busy fighting battles.

Now I have decided to stand for the Council of the National Trust. It is not that I have a vendetta against the National Trust, I have been visiting their properties for years – well, the Farne Islands – when I haven't been left waiting on the quay because of high winds and rough seas, which was the story of my visit this June. No, my problem with the National Trust is that the organisation seems to be more worried at the moment about buildings and tourists, than working people and thriving communities. In other words visitors and theme parks seem to take precedence over a living and working countryside.

My concern started when the Countryside Restoration Trust became interested in the two hill farms for sale on Snowdon. When the NT's appeal was launched with the implication that Snowdon was a 'playground', rather than a piece of working countryside that welcomed visitors, my heart sank.

Since then I have been to several parts of the country where the National Trust has large holdings. On Exmoor I have seen hedges with posters adorning them saying; 'You can't trust the National Trust' and in the Lakes I have met farmers at their financial wits end, who have had their rents raised by twenty five after their incomes had fallen by fifty percent. Men in suits with no roots and no culture have been telling people without suits, but with roots and culture how to run their lives.

It seems astonishing to me that as farming incomes fall, farmers are told to pay more rent and their wives, who are already raising families and working on the land, instructed that they should take in bed and breakfast visitors to cover the extra charges. How many of the men in suits suggest to their wives that they must take in bed and breakfast to make ends meet. And all this is going on as piles of wool burn and ewes cannot be given away. One of the early benefactors of the National Trust, Beatrix Potter, would be horrified. She saw the farmers, the rural communities and the Herdwick sheep as all being integral parts of the gift; now they are seen almost as inconveniences.

As part of my concern I visited the National Trust's offices in Cirencester. There I was told that only one tenant in the Lakes had received a rent increase; on my next trip north the first half-dozen farmers I met all claimed that their rents had gone up too.

But surely the National Trust is big enough, with considerable commercial clout to actually be leading their tenants out of hardship. With imagination and innovation there could be National Trust carpets, made from Herdwick fleeces; National Trust quality meat using local slaughterhouses instead of the animals travelling hundreds of miles and then being sold as 'Freedom Food' in Tesco. Because of the size of its land holding the National Trust could and should be leading the fight for its regional family farmers.

Similarly it should be changing attitudes in farming techniques. Time and time again I see hedges flailed in August and September and silage made in April on National Trust farms. Blame is put on existing tenancy agreements – but why not reduce the rent for those farmers who are environmentally aware? Yes, buildings and landscapes are fine; but it is people and communities who should be at the hub of National Trust policies – that is why I'm standing for the National Trust Council, it is as simple as that.

*Needless to say I lost – thanks to the Chairman's proxy votes.

17

Going, Going Gone

A mistle thrush is singing from the very top of a nearby ash tree. I used to regard the 'mavis' as a harbinger of spring; that distinctive piping melody heralding change before most other birds had recognised the approach of a new season. Today I feel differently; as its song comes into my study it brings with it memories, melancholy and deep sadness. As the seasons once passed, with every new flower, bird and butterfly, the phone would ring and Gordon Beningfield, the artist, would burst into enthusiastic celebration – the song of the mistle thrush, the first orange tip butterfly, the cuckoo.

It is strange how, that as time passes, I miss his wise counsel and his enthusiasm more and more. How lucky he was to miss Blair and Labour's vision for the countryside. But melancholy goes deeper still. Over the last three years I have lost five of the six most important and influential people in my life and he was one of them. One after the other they have gone; some after full and happy lives, some taken early with still so much to give, and now the sixth, the one remaining, has simply walked away and out of my life. It is a hard thing to reason or to fathom but that is what has happened.

The last five years have formed what has probably been the most important period of my life. It has been a time when the Countryside Restoration Trust grew faster and achieved more than I could have possibly imagined. It has been a roller-coaster of a ride of success and disappointment, laughter and tears; an election was fought for a lost cause, marches were joined, points were made and the skylark was brought back to part of Cambridgeshire's prairies. As some of those who inspired the battles and shared the ups and downs left the field, Margaret was always there; smiling at the successes; sharing in the grief of the departures.

It was an unexpected meeting, she arriving at my door wanting a part-time secretarial job after reading of the piles of unanswered letters in my study. Her help made little difference because as the CRT grew she became its first paid employee and many of my letters remained waiting for attention. Other things grew too and it was in the Falklands that we became engaged, in the famous Upland Goose Hotel. Sadly none of the shops in Port Stanley had a ring to fit and so we marked the promise with a rubber band carefully wrapped around the fourth finger of her left hand. A proper ring followed, carefully selected with help from Gordon Beningfield at the Annual Shire Horse Show at Peterborough. It was a beautiful, simple ring – three rings in one.

It was an unexpected event in my life, springing out of nowhere; the end has been just as unexpected. I began writing *The Hunting Gene* about a year ago. It seemed to me important on a number of levels, involving civil liberties, conservation, wildlife and indeed animal welfare. As a non-hunter but as a countryman it also seemed important as a part of rural culture. Astonishingly, after twenty-three books, and after being courted by a main-stream publisher, suddenly, at the mention of a book on hunting, publishers and editors fled with their hands raised in horror.

Similarly the BBC and Channel 4 found the idea of televised political incorrectness too much to contemplate.

It seemed to me that this was a form of censorship by the very people who usually advocated freedom of speech. The BBC it seemed could be very exercised about the 'rights' of Salman Rushdie, but they were not very troubled about the 'rights' of an English peasant. So I decided to publish the book myself; the rest of my life, house extensions, what to do about the farm with my brother retiring, the replacement for my little dog would all have to go on hold; if the hunting argument had to be put, it was now, before another Private Member's Bill and/or abolition. I thought Margaret would understand, after all she hunted, as a whipper-in with the Granta Harriers.

I was wrong. There followed the most physically and emotionally demanding period of my life; to get *The Hunting Gene* completed – and I only just beat yet another Private Member's Bill, and the deadline for evidence to the Burns Inquiry – took thousands of miles, working seven days a week for between fifteen and eighteen hours a day. For me it was a matter of principle and as the book came together the work seemed worth it. With wonderful illustrations and some marvellous experiences it looked as if I could produce a good book to make an honest case for hunting, conservation and the country way of life.

At the end of the exercise I was and am exhausted – so are my life savings. I have a shirt, a roof and two thousand pounds to my name, but I also have a book I can feel proud of and I have done my best. But that is all I have; my intended marriage is over, for as I a non-hunter defended hunting, Margaret was hunting elsewhere. As my pounds turned to pence, she found an intensive farmer with several acres of building land; planning appeal seemed to triumph over peasant appeal and it feels as if five important years have been taken from me.

It has been a devastating and bitter pill to swallow; the plot of real life has resembled a modern Thomas Hardy novel, with gloom, doom and disaster at every turn. The final twist coming last Friday, the arrival of the completed book coinciding with a note from Margaret in my letterbox saying she had married. This brings me back to the melancholy song of the thrush, still singing, the 'Darkling Thrush', and Gordon Beningfield. He was a self taught expert on Thomas Hardy; but he would have been saddened by this story, this plot and this ending. Ironically the last bird painting in his last book was of a mistle thrush. When he so tragically died he was working on another book, one that he felt deeply about, it was to be called 'Beningfield's Vanishing Songbirds'; the unfinished painting that he was working on at the end of his struggle was a song thrush.

After disappointment, trauma and tears life goes on. I now want to produce another book. I want to finish 'Beningfield's Vanishing Songbirds' as a tribute to a good man and a loyal friend.

18

Conservation Antiquities

———

The recent Countryside Live event at Syon Park in London was interesting. It demonstrated just how huge the gulf between town and country has become. On the Friday hundreds of children were enjoying themselves with their first taste of the countryside. It did not matter that some were terrified at being within touching distance of a sheep, or that some children asked if the fox hounds were pigs. It did not matter either that there were children present who had no idea where milk comes from. The good news was that they were there, they were learning and enjoying from first hand practical experience.

This began a very worrying thought process. If most modern children are cut off from nature and wildlife, where will the next generation of countryside keepers and conservationists come from? It is a disturbing thought. Nearly all the great advances in conservation over recent decades have been made by self-taught amateur naturalists, all with a sense of mission and vision gained from their knowledge of the wild. With fewer young people in touch with nature it could mean that wildlife and conservation will simply become another university option and wildlife conservation will be seen as an area of 'management options' for scientists, environmental studies graduates and bureaucrats.

The simple facts are, that all the significant conservationists and naturalists that I have been privileged to meet, have been self-taught. George Adamson with his lions in Kenya was either ignored or ridiculed by the wildlife establishment, yet he made a massive contribution to our knowledge of releasing animals back into the wild.

Similarly today, in this country the scientific establishment look down their noses at the work of John Aspinall. But facts speak louder than jealousies and the facts are that by using common sense and knowledge, rather than scientific bluff and bluster, John Aspinall has managed to breed gorillas, tigers, African elephants, black rhino and the rare bongo antelope, where many scientists have failed.

In much the same way the return of the otter to much of Britain is often dismissed by scientists. What few of them admit is that the return is largely due to the captive breeding and release programmes of Philip Wayre, founder of the Otter Trust – needless to say Philip is a self-taught non-scientist.

Even the great Dame, Miriam Rothschild, is largely self-taught and her work on hay meadows, butterflies, dragonflies etc. is without equal. Even now she is working on various schemes for hedgerows and field margins and trying to interest farmers in her work. Then of course there another conservation hero, David Bellamy; he started out as a laboratory technician but has become the most effective conservation communicator of them all.

Finally I have to remind readers, that it was in 1980 that the late Gordon Beningfield cajoled me into accompanying him to the RSPB to fight for farmland birds and wildlife – all to no avail. Then, we made even most amateur naturalists look professional by comparison. A few years later, with wise words of encouragement from Sir Laurens van der Post, the Countryside Restoration

Trust was born – out of the blindness of scientists, professional conservationists and bureaucrats.

In Norfolk too there is a remarkable amateur naturalist who has achieved much. The work of Bill Makins can be seen at the Pensthorpe Waterfowl Park near Fakenham. Bill started his wildlife work adventurously in Africa, then, on being given a clutch of tufted duck eggs an interest in wildfowl was hatched. He collected eggs in Chile, Alaska, Siberia and Spain, quite legally and often in areas threatened with drainage and development. As a result the gravel workings on his farm became one of the most spectacular wildfowl breeding centres in Europe. Wild species have moved in too; kingfishers, teal, shoveller and many more. In addition he has ideas for the captive breeding and release of the corncrake and the European crane. Sadly, these schemes have attracted hardly any interest from the scientific establishment, presumably because the scientists did not think of them first.

Bill is now retiring, at the age of 68 he has fallen into too many rivers and bogs to keep going at his present speed and the 500 acres of Pensthorpe with its wonderful wildlife is up for sale. This brings me back to children. Pensthorpe is exactly the kind of place where today's generation of children could actually be inspired and put back in touch with nature. If I win the lottery I think Pensthorpe would be on my shopping list for about £2m. It would make an ideal headquarters for the CRT too. Perhaps it is about time I bought a ticket.

19

Small, Brown and Beautiful

———

At last there is good news in my life. The sun is warm, the world is bright and I am in love again – with a meadow pipit. Yes, this little brown job, seen by the thousand on moorland, marsh and heath has become my favourite bird. I have been aware of meadow pipits for years; I associate them with trips away from Cambridgeshire to Dartmoor, Exmoor, the Lakes and some of Britain's most attractive landscapes. It is the meadow pipit's lot to be a major food source for the merlin and the kestrel. It can't be much fun being brown, boring and a major food source.

My love affair started when I was walking across the middle of the CRT's Lark Rise Farm in Cambridgeshire. There, sitting on a piece of bamboo marker in the middle of a newly planted hedge was a meadow pipit, at the end of May? Then I saw another – and another. Meadow pipits in May? I was astonished; I had seen flocks of meadow pipits pass through in winter before, but had never seen them in the summer. This could only mean one thing – they were breeding on Lark Rise Farm. I was staggered; meadow pipits breeding on farmland in Cambridgeshire, if I had not seen it for myself I would have found it hard to believe. I was so amazed that I phoned the great pundit on breeding birds, the BTO's Chris Mead. 'Yes, Robin', he said, 'it is unusual for them to breed on ordinary farmland, but not rare'. So not for the first time in my life I was becoming excited by the unusual – medium but not rare. Then came a shock. The Breeding Bird Report for Lark Rise Farm, for 1999, conducted by the British Trust for Ornithology, plopped through my letter box. The BTO is an excellent organisation, doing much good work, and there in the Report on breeding territories '3 Meadow Pipit'. I could not believe my eyes. Three territories for 1999 – this meant that it took me a whole year to notice my new loves – it was a cause of both joy and acute embarrassment. The Report confirmed numerous farmland birds doing disastrously nationally but thriving on Lark Rise Farm. We had breeding grey partridge, yellow wagtail, song thrush, corn bunting, hobby, yellowhammer, reed bunting, linnet, blackbird, skylark, and yes, meadow pipit and many more. Appropriately, the skylark was the most numerous species with good numbers of yellowhammers, reed buntings and whitethroats. It means we are doing several things right for conservation, while at the same time growing good crops. The whole thing is most encouraging, for me, for the CRT, for farming and conservation. Needless to say, it is so encouraging that Nick Brown, the Secretary of State for Agriculture, still has not been to see what we are doing. Never mind, another invitation will shortly be issued to him, to see if we can lure the worst Minister of State ever to venture north of the M25.

I hope, despite the negative effect on life of our present batch of awful politicians, that I can keep my enthusiasm going until I am ninety-two. Last week I went with a carload of farmers to the Great Dame of British conservation, Miriam Rothschild. Normally she has an annual party for conservationists. This year she had one for farmers. Like the CRT, and she became our first honorary life member, she believes that the future of conservation in this country, if not the world, depends on farmers and farmland. So brimming over with enthusiasm she invited a house full of farmers to eat, drink and look at her hay meadows, her hedgerows and her field margins, followed after lunch by an excellent presentation by the Game Conservancy, so I am told. As usual after a good meal as soon as my posterior hit a chair I fell asleep and missed all the stuff about getting lapwings back. I am assured however, that it was very interesting – between my snores.

In between all this two press releases arrived from the BTO. I am quite sincere in my admiration for the BTO – and the RSPB. My only criticism is that they are both afflicted by 'conservational correctness'. The first release was a list of disasters. Numbers of yellowhammers, linnets, reed buntings, and yes, the meadow pipit were crashing with specific reference to 'failure at egg stage', 'incubation stage failures' etc. In other words the eggs and nests were being raided.

The second press release was entitled 'Britain in the Third Millennium; Heaven for Crows?' It stated how well carrion crows and magpies were doing and it gave various reasons for this, except the obvious one related to the first press release – dining on the eggs and young of reed buntings, yellowhammers, meadow pipits and many more. I phoned the BTO headquarters – I could not bear to phone Chris Mead in case he came out with the wrong answers. The gentleman who answered had no idea why the nests and eggs had failed: ' The eggs could have been eaten after the nest was abandoned', he said, without conviction. Sorry, that is the wrong answer. Predation by magpies and crows is one – only one- of the main reasons for the tragic decline in farmland birds. Come on BTO and RSPB – put conservation and the welfare of birds before 'conservational correctness' and tell us the truth.

20

The Hounded

The sun shone, the day was warm, men, women and children were happy, smiling and talkative. There was the sound of hounds barking, and friends were laughing and chatting about old times, good times and times to come. I was at the South of England Hound Show at Ardingly in Sussex – I think. The hound show is a show within a show – part of the South of England Show – the farming community's south of England farming festival. It seemed better than the East of England Show – not so many double-glazing and teddy bear salesmen.

I was selling copies of *The Hunting Gene* as usual, and enjoying it. Now that I have broken even on this politically incorrect venture I have the equivalent of eighteen months back pay to make up.

Until I started writing the book I had never been to a hound show. It is one of life's pleasures that had passed me by. My summer Saturday afternoons had always been taken up with cricket and I had never heard of the great hound shows at Ardingly, Peterborough, Harrogate, Lowther, Rydal and Honiton.

Hound shows are exactly what they imply: shows to find the top hound, bitch, dog, puppy and couple. Almost all over

England hounds are counted in pairs, 'couples', except in the Lake District, there, so I am told, they count the feet and divide by four.

At Ardingly I took particular interest in what was going on as I have been invited to judge at two hound shows during the summer, at the Puckeridge Foxhounds and the Quantock Staghounds. This is interesting as I know nothing about the finer points of hound physiology and I shall simply pick what to me is the prettiest hound with the happiest eyes. Apparently wearing a bowler hat makes the decision-making process more simple and helps clarify the thought processes. Consequently I shall dig out my long departed grandfather's bowler hat and another great milestone in the journey of life will have been achieved: hound show judge.

Hounds are wonderful dogs – loyal, intelligent, friendly, brave and always hungry. The trick at a hound show is to make the beast behave at its best by making it look at, and then chase a dog biscuit. Grown men in smart hunt uniforms were twiddling biscuits and the hounds performed perfectly. The East Kent Foxhounds won an armful of rosettes, and at each announcement the huntsman's wife, smiling, happy and built for comfort, squealed with delight from the recesses of the grandstand.

All day long I had a succession of people buying books, from peers to postmen. In exactly the same way as cricket, hunting covers the entire social spectrum. 'What is going to happen?' they all asked. 'Will the politicians take notice of the Burns Report?' I had to reply that I had no idea; the bulk of our politicians these days are career men – conviction has been replaced by ego-tripping expediency.

One elderly man asked me why I was no longer on the BBC's 'Question Time' or 'Any Questions' as the country viewpoint is never heard. I had to tell him that after a three-year lay-off, I have been invited back onto 'Any Questions' in Exeter – very handy from my Cambridgeshire home. But as far as 'Question Time' is concerned I am still in outer-darkness. After a successful first programme I was then told that I would not be back as I was 'anti-Europe': 'We wanted you as a countryman, not as an anti-European' they told me. It is totally beyond the comprehension of the BBC's political elite that most countrymen are anti-Europe because of the damage done to the countryside by the Common Agricultural Policy.

The next day dawned grey and wet. The mood of the people for the Beagle Show had changed too. Incredibly, the Home Secretary, Jack Straw, has suddenly announced a parliamentary Bill on hunting before he has even received the Burns Report on hunting with dogs. Consequently a supposedly consensual government has become a dictatorial government showing total contempt for the democratic process of information and discussion, before decision.

The book still sold, the beagles still chased their biscuits; but there was an air of gloom and despondency. One old lady, on the verge of tears, came to talk; the countryside from farms to fields, horses and hounds, chestnuts to chutney had been her life; now it was to be taken away from her. That is what the politicians, the clever Dicks, the BBC, cannot understand – that an attack on hunting is an attack on the personal lives and freedoms of ordinary traditional country people.

As I have written many times before, I do not hunt, shoot or fish, but I love the traditional countryside and traditional country people. Because of this I get the feeling that soon I will achieve another great milestone in the journey of life: I will become a prisoner. I will become a political prisoner of Tony Blair – Denim Man – and his politically correct cronies, simply for standing up for freedom and the countryside I love.

21

The Lazy Days of Summer

––––

It had been a long day. I had left the house at six o'clock in the morning to sell copies of my book at the South of England Show. I had then driven to a small stone village near Stow on the Wold to address the Cotswold branch of the CPRE. I arrived home at 1.45 am the next day to find eleven stored messages on my answerphone. The last one was the most important: 'Watt Tyler', it said, 'you are wanted in Parliament Square on Monday for a silent protest against this despicable Government'.

I do not like demonstrating; I do not like going to London at this time of year, I prefer to be under larksong, working, or looking for wildflowers and butterflies. But in reality there is no choice; with farming under increasing attack, with rural communities falling apart and now with hunting the focus of discrimination, ignorance and bigotry, I would have to go to London to protest about the cultural cleansing of the British countryside.

Twelve hours later came another request: 'Watt, will you address the masses in Parliament Square?' Again I felt I had no option, although I did warn that I may have to sit down in the road immediately afterwards out of sheer fatigue.

Saturday evening, still car-lagged, I attended the Cambridgeshire Hunt Ball. It was held on the farm of a friend. As young men neither of us hunted, we played village football on

Saturday afternoons. When his footballing days were over he became a non-riding, non-hunting Master of Hounds, simply because he did not like the dishonesty and aggression of those who opposed hunting. Hunt Balls are not the elite social gatherings they are made out to be. They are events for eating, drinking and laughing with friends. Alas between the meal and the horn blowing competition I had to halt the laughter and urge attendance at Parliament Square.

Monday dawned; it was a beautiful day. As I watered my sheep, using a bucket on a piece of cord, thrown into the brook, I heard the purring call of a turtledove – only the second one of the summer. I did not want to go to London. However, principle is more important than convenience when basic freedoms and the continuance of rural culture are at stake.

I travelled by train with Nigel Housden who took many of the photographs for *The Hunting Gene*. Before doing the book he had absolutely no interest in hunting. Since meeting the hunting people of the Lakes, Exmoor and the Cotswolds; since seeing the horses and the hounds and after seeing the landscape and conservation links with hunting, he, like me is outraged at what is happening to the traditional country people of rural Britain.

At the time of the Countryside Rally and March, London was full of country people. On this occasion we appeared to be the only ones, attracting stares and suspicious glances. In a pub in Whitehall we found some others. What a relief; we were not on our own. Police came in, obviously counting. We moved on to Parliament Square.

There were ordinary working class people I recognised from Manchester and Yorkshire, and working farmers from Exmoor and Cambridgeshire. I recognised accents too from the valleys of Wales and the fells of the Lakes. All at virtually no notice, at their own expense, had downed tools to rush to London. As usual the BBC – the Blair Broadcasting Corporation – counted 1000 protesters; there were at least 2500.

Then I saw some real 'toffs'; smooth suited, anti-hunting MP's. 'Get out of the way' one elitist growled as he barged me aside, kicking me as he did so. If I had retaliated I would have been the one in prison for assault. They were almost caricatures from Westminster's chattering classes – men in suits without roots, without culture and with no wildlife telling men without suits, but with roots, with culture and with wildlife how to run their lives. Hear the chattering classes on the subject of 'Missionaries'; how it is wrong for one culture to be imposed on another. Yet these same ego-tripping chatterers want to impose their values and culture on country people.

Law abiding people are embarrassed to protest. Horns were blown, chants shouted; it was the noisiest 'silent protest' I had ever witnessed. I addressed the throng from a lamppost – shouting, as microphones are not allowed near the House of Commons – no longer the Mother of Parliaments – the Mother of vindictiveness and discrimination. I wanted to wave *The Hunting Gene* at Parliament – sadly it could not be done hanging onto a lamppost. We sat in the road – 'Should we be doing this,' said an Exmoor lady, 'It will give a bad impression'. The throng then marched to Millbank, Labour's Headquarters and policy centre. The airless tower had anti-hunting posters on the inside, showing Jack Straw's phony impartiality. An effigy of Tony Blair was hung in a tree and the crowd dispersed.

In a pub afterwards the talk was of tractors in the streets; Manchester and London gridlocked, civil disobedience and prison. I too will be prepared to go to prison for these people and for the countryside I love. Tragically Labour seems to have become new Labour – new Blair – new fascism.

22

Better Late Than Never

———

For several weeks now I have received a number of letters querying, questioning and complaining about the RSPB's recent announcement that it is to buy 'Hope Farm'. The farm, on Cambridgeshire clay is to be farmed with wildlife in mind and the literature concerning the purchase is liberally adorned with skylarks. Don't they know, my correspondents enquire, of the work of The Countryside Restoration Trust, whose logo of course is a skylark? Some writers go even further and ask why the BBC's supposed countryside programme, 'Countryfile' managed to deal in some detail with 'Hope Farm', but has managed to avoid any mention of the CRT's 'Lark Rise Farm', for six and a half years.

As founder and Chairman of the Countryside Restoration Trust, whose initial land purchases were made possible largely by the generous donations of ordinary people, I do not have a problem with the RSPB's new project. I regard it as a huge compliment that such a large organisation has decided to follow in our footsteps – and those of the Game Conservancy – and I believe that with its greater resources it will be able to benefit from the work we have already done, and complement the work that we are still doing.

On a personal basis I have a very good relationship with the RSPB. I like many individual members of staff; I have regular exchanges of views with them; the organisation has achieved much valuable conservation work and I have been a fully paid-up member since the 1950s; it cannot give me the exact date as the record keeping in those days obviously left something to be desired. Most years Graham Wynne, the Chief Executive and former chief Barbara Young – Baroness Young of Old Scone (not Fruit Cake), meet me either on CRT land, or at an RSPB reserve to talk about conservation problems in the general countryside. Another meeting is to be scheduled for either this month or next. I like both of them, although Barbara Young does have a few 'Blair Babe' tendencies, which, I am sure with perseverance and the right treatment can be cured. Indeed she did excellent work at the RSPB and is now like a breath of fresh air at the Environment Agency.

However, everything the RSPB and English Nature get involved with does not always smell of roses. The RSPB has a problem with size, as does any large organisation, and its head-quarters staff can sometimes be out of step with its staff on the ground – particularly on the need to control predators. On the same problem, the RSPB does seem to be very conservationally correct on the need to control magpies, crows, foxes, sparrowhawks and hen harriers, for fear of upsetting those of its members influenced by Rolf Harris and the 'Bambi syndrome'. In addition, although it boasts of the quality of its science, when a recent scientific report clearly implicated hen harriers and peregrines for devastating a grouse moor, that science was either ignored or distorted.

So, on the whole I haven't a problem with the RSPB and welcome its involvement in farming. Some readers will remember that the late Gordon Beningfield, actually took me with him to the RSPB in 1980. We pleaded with the then Chief Executive for the RSPB to become involved with farming and the general countryside, but we failed to make any impression. Ian Presst stated clearly that the future of conservation was with nature reserves and Sites of Special Scientific Interest; the meeting left us both very depressed and the creation of the Countryside Restoration Trust was the eventual result. So it has taken the RSPB nearly twenty years to catch up, so how can I be anything but pleased? All we need now is for 'Countryfile' to catch up.

Already too the CRT has some interesting links with the RSPB's new project. Roger Buisson of the RSPB will be in charge of the scheme and he has been helping to monitor birds on the

CRT's Lark Rise Farm for over a year. In addition the RSPB's land is to be contract farmed by the Co-op. The contract farmer appointed is a young Welshman, Martin Davies, who has achieved much good work on nearby Co-op land. In addition he is married to my cousin – who unfairly has scooped nearly all the family's 'beauty genes' – and she serves on the Management Committee of the CRT, so we hope that all the good results we have achieved will help to benefit the RSPB initiative. Our results can, at the moment, be seen in assorted feathers and fur; the CRT land is currently awash with wildlife, skylarks, reed buntings, corn buntings, English partridges, harvest mice and brown hares. The otters that originally launched us into action are also still regular visitors.

It would have made more sense for the RSPB's new land to have been further away from the CRT – it is about six miles distance as the crow flies, but never mind. In addition, and without diminishing the conservation and farming abilities of Martin Davies, I believe that the RSPB should have put a family into the farm, either as tenants, or managers. Conservation cannot take place on a farm without the farmers making a living and a profit, and this should be just as important in the RSPB's equation as skylarks.

By an ironic twist I believe that the most benefit to be gained from the RSPB's purchase of Hope Farm will be on the subject of predation. At the Game Conservancy's farm at Loddington in Leicestershire, wildlife has flooded back with both habitat management and predator control. At the CRT's Lark Rise Farm wildlife is flooding back through habitat management and second hand predator control – land owners surrounding us control magpies with Larson traps, and crows and foxes with rifles, and our wildlife benefits as a direct result.

Dr. Mark Avery, the RSPB's Director of Conservation, claims to be a doubter on the effect of predation and often starts his talks with the odd sentence 'Speaking as a Scientist', as if that gives some justification for some of his more curious views. I hope that after a few years work on Hope Farm, with no control of crows, magpies and foxes – all currently thriving on the farm – that Dr.

Avery will give us the whole story of the farm's farmland birds: 'As a scientist'. In addition of course, no Larson traps, or snares, must be set just off the RSPB land, as has happened, so it is claimed, around some RSPB reserves – that is bad practice and misleading science.

23

Disenchanted – Disenfranchised

———

I am in no way trying to jump on any sort of band wagon, but I have always loved the W.I. I have spoken to large groups and small groups of them. I have eaten chutney, sung *Jerusalem* and judged the cake competition, taking two slices on some occasions to ensure the accuracy of my taste buds. My cousin is an ex-President, and another ex-President, evidently feeling sorry for the peasant classes, regularly gives me home-made lemon curd tarts. On no occasion have I ever been heckled or slow hand-clapped by these wonderful discerning people. The only thing I do not understand about their recent treatment of Mr. Blair is, why did it take so long for them to see that the Emperor had no clothes, and why did it take so long for everybody else to follow suit?

I have to say that I was no fan of John Major, who I regarded as the most effective and natural non-leader ever to gain the leadership of the Conservative Party. But once the electorate had quite rightly got rid of him, it took me approximately a fortnight to see through Denim Man, Tuscany Tony – Tony Blair. Indeed several months ago now the Editor of 'Weekend' phoned to say; 'Robin, you'll have to do another Diary, we simply cannot print the one you have written about Tony Blair'. I was rather disappointed; I considered it to be a restrained piece about the man who is systematically destroying farming and rural culture in this country.

But all this creates a problem, for who is there for the country-man, or countrywoman, to vote for at the moment? The answer is nobody – like hundreds of thousands of others I am effectively disfranchised. My dilemma was demonstrated perfectly at the Royal Show last week. I know that two years ago I said I would never go to Stoneleigh again because I had all the double glazing and teddy bears that I needed, but the Countryside Alliance said 'Come and sell your book on our stand' and for the sake of diversification I felt compelled to accept.

I have never known the mood of farmers and country people to have turned as it has today. It has gone beyond depression and frustration and it is turning into raw anger – there is a mood of civil disobedience and rebellion in the air; the farming and rural communities feel betrayed by their politicians, their parliament and their union representatives.

Nick Brown, the Minister of MAFF, was at the Royal Show (the Ministry Against Farming and Foxhunting). Like a frightened rabbit he scurried from Establishment pavilion to Establishment pavilion, with his Establishment minders ensuring that he did not meet any real farmers or farmworkers. Dressed in a fetching brown suit the unfortunate Mr. Brown cut a sad figure – sad for farming that is – how on earth can a politician who appears to be so inarticulate, urban and agriculturally and countryside illiterate be in charge of the activity that shapes the countryside and our rural communities? If you destroy farming and rural communities you destroy the very soul of the countryside, and that is exactly what this Labour Government is doing.

But where can we turn? Tim Yeo, the shadow MAFF mullah was also present. At least he was out and about meeting real people unlike Nick Frightened Rabbit. But what had he got to offer and how can the Tories 'save our countryside', when they started the rot in the first place? I asked how he was going to save farming when it was the Tories who, at the instruction of Brussels, had allowed cereal prices to fall to world levels. It was the Tories who ruined livestock farming with their inept handling of BSE and it was the Tories who, at the instruction of Brussels, deregulated milk, by dismantling the Milk Marketing Board, and who caused the current crisis in dairy farming. All he could answer was that the Tories would fight red tape. That is rich, as they created most of it in the first place and Frightened Rabbit has been adding to it ever since.

I do not know whether the Liberal Democrats were at the Royal Show, and I am not really interested. A few weeks ago the Lib-Dem leader (I am sorry, he is so charismatic I cannot remember his name) made noises that sounded environmentally green. I wrote him a letter congratulating him and inviting him to expand his case. A quite extraordinary letter came back, full of wind, waffle and nothing of substance – all about access to the countryside and managing it for the benefit of all – nothing about solving the countryside crisis or saving rural culture.

So who can we turn to for help? It seems to me that we must start helping ourselves; we must take a leaf out of the French farmer's book. I am getting my marching boots out again and oiling my muck spreader, if country people are going to get sidelined and treated with discrimination then we must do what any other minority would do. The only trouble with this policy is that already *Horse and Hound* have made me and my colleague Willy Poole 6 to 4 on favourites to be the first in prison. Sharing a cell with Willy Poole? I fear that is a price too high to pay.

24

A Sigh for Songbirds

———

For generations birds and people have lived side by side and, as I start this chapter I am being watched by nine house sparrows (yes, I still have them), two hedge sparrows and a robin, all in a forsythia bush in front my window. For hundreds of generations we have lived close to birds; we have watched them, listened to them and even eaten them. They have been, and should still be, part of our lives. As a result, they have been celebrated in poetry, painting and music, although today, the sound of Vaughan Williams' 'The Lark Ascending' is often more common than the song of the skylark itself.

Because of our close association with birds, we also need them. For two million years our ancestors lived surrounded by nature. In fact, they were part of nature and depended on it for their survival. Then, for ten thousand years we were farmers when a variety of wild birds joined us in and around the farms and homesteads. It is only in the last fifty years that massive urbanisation has separated us from our past, and separated us from nature; that is why we like birds, and that is why the RSPB is the largest bird conservation charity in the world. Birds, and songbirds in particular, give us the feeling that we are still in touch with nature. We love to hear the song of the skylark and the nightingale; we welcome, or at least some sensible people do, the return of the swallow to our garages and the swift to our attics, and it is a joy to see the robin on the bird table and the blue tit on the peanuts. Our enthusiasm for birds was demonstrated perfectly during the week, when a survey announced on the 'Today' programme about swifts and swallows nesting in houses and gardens, resulted in over 7000 hits on the RSPB's web site before the programme was even over. But make the best of it while you can – many bird species are in steep decline and many of our best loved birds are quite literally in free-fall.

In the last twenty-five years the populations of some of our best loved birds have plummeted; the tree sparrow by 87%, house sparrow 58%, English partridge 82%, starling 82%, yellowhammer 43%, skylark 52%, linnet 38%, song thrush 55%, swallow 16% and the cuckoo 12%. This year too, there has been a crash in the population of swifts and in the spring I only heard the cuckoo in two short bursts.

Many of the reasons for the continuing disaster are obvious and nearly all of them are man made. Courtesy of the Common

Agricultural Policy, farming is still becoming an industrial process, instead of a partnership between man and nature – the 'culture' is being taken out of agriculture. Hedges and rough places are still being lost for 'tidiness' and 'efficiency'; this means nesting areas and shelter are being destroyed and insects – the food of many wild birds – have nowhere to live, feed and breed. In addition to this, over hundreds of thousands of acres, organophosphate chemicals are used on cultivated crops, killing all the insects for days on end, meaning that swallows, skylarks and partridges have nothing on which to feed their young.

In hill areas, 'Ivermectin', a chemical that kills worms in livestock can remain active for up to three days in cow-pats and sheep droppings, again affecting insect populations. Slug pellets in crops and gardens mean the removal of slugs and snails, the staple diet of the much-loved song thrush.

Farmyards themselves are now so clean and tidy that there is no mud for swallows to make their nests, and no spilled corn for sparrows to eat. To make matters worse, many farmers are now being required to join 'Assured cereals' schemes. These set out to guarantee cleanliness and 'traceability' in a health obsessed society. To belong to a scheme, all birds have to be kept out of buildings, meaning that the swallow and the barn owl have nowhere to nest. That is why I buy no food claiming to be 'assured' – I would rather eat bread containing the odd cooked swallow dropping, than bread produced at the expense of one of the world's most attractive and remarkable birds.

Development and tidying again lead to lost habitat. Only last week at the Cambridge University Vet. College it is alleged that buildings were levelled containing nesting swallows. Not only did this break the Wildlife and Countryside Act, but it also sets such a bad example. All over the south-east similar examples of swift and swallow sites being lost are being reported. At the same time thousands of new houses are being built without ledges and eaves required for nesting summer visitors. John Prescott should be doing something about this, but having him as Secretary of State for the Environment is rather like making Bernard Manning Secretary of State for Culture.

In ordinary gardens too, weedkillers, slug pellets and tidiness are destroying habitat for birds. In addition, garden sheds and garages are kept locked and some people still knock down the nests of house martins, quite illegally, as they don't want the 'mess' – I wish I was lucky enough to have that mess.

There are still more hazards out there. As many of our bird numbers have fallen, predator numbers have risen. Magpies have increased by 113%, Carrion Crows by 120% and Sparrowhawks by 162%. It is incredible. If a deer eats a rare plant, it is shot and nobody says a word, yet if anybody suggests controlling the out of control sparrowhawk for eating rare birds, conservation bodies all express outrage. Perhaps the Royal Society for the Protection of Birds should change its name to the Royal Society for the Conservation of Birds, it might then take a more realistic view.

Then there is the cat problem – an estimated nine million cats kill up to 240 million animals and birds a year. Our two farm kittens are already killing young robins and sparrows with frightening efficiency, and it is my belief that the figure of 240,000,000 is an underestimate.

But the good news is that the impending disaster can be turned around. I feed my garden birds all the year round, including wheat sprinkled on the ground. As a result I have a healthy sparrow population. On the farm the sparrowhawks killed the last of our swallows but I am determined to get them back too. In 1993 with the now sadly departed Sir Laurens van der Post and the artist Gordon Beningfield, I launched the Countryside Restoration Trust, with the intention of getting wildlife and farming back in harmony. Already on the Trust's 250 acre Lark Rise Farm in Cambridgeshire we have seen the return of skylarks galore, English partridges, corn buntings, house sparrows, yellowhammers, reed bunting and yellow wagtails. Given the chance, nature, including some of our best loved birds, can be restored. We must give them that chance.

25

One Man And His Corset

———

The pace of life changes so constantly that I never seem to know what is going to happen next. Well, something drastic and unexpected has just happened and as a result my whole life style has had to adjust. I do not want to shock any delicate reader, but a beautiful young lady has just moved into my house with me and she has given me a new lease of life.

It was love at first sight; one of the most beautiful faces I have ever seen with deep dark eyes. I had better say too that she is black – brown and white – an absolutely stunning foxhound puppy. Yes, thanks to the likes of Miranda Blair and Michael Foster, for the first time in my life I have become a puppy walker, or at least I am being walked by a puppy.

As soon as Paul the kennelman opened the door of his van I knew it was a match made in heaven, apart from one thing. Now I know that I am not the most sylph-like of creatures, but why was I given a puppy called 'Corset'? The name has other dangers too; now, as I walk down the road shouting 'Corset, Corset', ladies with wild rolling eyes swivel on their heels and scowl at me, seething with indignation.

The name is a shame as Corset's mother was called 'Cobweb' and a sister is 'Cowslip'. Corset is so unfair for a hound so elegant and beautiful. If hunting really is the sport of 'Toffs' as some believe, perhaps I should make Corset's name more toff-like. She could become Corset-Bambi; one of the Corset-Bambis of Upper Cambridgeshire. Her diet and personal habits are far from toff-like. Her first meal in my house consisted of tea bags turfed out of the waste bin. She gulped them down – mouthfuls of used PG Tips. If she had been a toff she would only have eaten Earl Grey.

So far, for the benefit of all those who are already saying: 'There you are, foxhounds can be house-trained', she has ripped up one rug; she has kept all the neighbours awake for three nights; she has climbed the stairs and howled blue murder because she daren't come down again; she has taken over my favourite armchair; the chaos caused has made me miss two article deadlines and she passes wind with an abandon that I have not experienced since I was twelve at the annual boy scout camp.

The first time Corset took me for a walk was remarkable. We walked along the hay meadows of the CRT's Telegraph Field. For the first ten or twelve years of my little lurcher Bramble's life, we walked the fields, tracks and driftways without seeing a single hare. Now, with Corset in tow, on just eight acres of grass we saw ten brown hares. They were a mixture of adults and threequarter grown leverets. If I had a lurcher now, to accompany Corset, life would be fraught. The lurcher would forever be disappearing into the distance after hares – crossing roads and crashing through hedges. As soon as one chaos would finish, another would start up. Currently there are some scientists getting large sums of money to investigate how to increase hare numbers. We have already found out the answers for nothing.

At the end of the meadow a hare got up and ran just in front of Corset. The puppy lolloped after it, only to almost tread on another; she screeched to a halt in alarm. Furry little animals should not be allowed to frighten young foxhounds like that.

Her favourite toy is a furry little animal – a psychedelic rainbow coloured rat that squeaks when bitten. This raises a serious moral question. Is it right to encourage pet dogs to savagely attack imitation furry animals, even if those furry animals are rainbow coloured? Surely such savage encouragement of both dogs and cats should be banned by Parliament. Instead pet dogs should be encouraged to play with imitation vegetables such as soya beans or potatoes, or trained to like miniature replicas of the patron saints of Petland, St. Paul McCartney and St. Rolf Harris.

I did see what I regarded as real cruelty the other day. While attending the Peterborough Hound Show at the East of England Showground, I visited the other end of the site to look at a conventional dog show. I was horrified. Dogs of all shapes and sizes were being shampooed, combed, sprayed and cosseted to look like 'things' rather than animals. Little carts and bootees were used to prevent the pampered beasts from getting their feet dirty. In addition there were doggie hairdryers and blowers and even electric dog walkers so that neither dog nor owner need leave the sitting room when going for 'walkies'. The owners looked largely urban, with gaudy jewellery to complement their pretty, living toys.

Corset is a beautiful dog, bred through hundreds of generations to work; to me, many of the show dogs, and some of the owners, were little more than freaks. I found the whole thing very sad and unpleasant. However, in a free country, I will not be urging Parliament to ban Crufts and all its offshoots. I will simply never go to such a show again; I hope that eventually people will become more civilised and that animal freak shows will become a thing of the past.

26

Snoring in the Morning

———

I suppose the first night with my new- found love was the beginning of my re-education. My last love was bad enough, with nightly snoring, plus a variety of violent twitches and wind symphonies. I am, of course, referring to my previous dog, but Corset's nocturnal melodies immediately reached new and dizzy musical heights. She cried, she howled, she whined, she barked, she scrapped, she growled and she emitted noises for which the English language has no name. The racket became so bad that I had to cover the kennel with blankets and close my bedroom window.

Still the cacophony for new love, or lost friends continued, penetrating my now closed windows and rebounding off the bedroom walls in great waves of wailing. It was so bad that I had to retreat. Collecting my night-cap, bed-socks and blankets I fled from the back of the house to the front- sorry – advanced and I closed the door behind me hoping for sleep in new found peace.

It is true that the melody of anguish could only just be heard, but I had forgotten how uncomfortable the spare bed had become. It is a very old bed; how many people have given birth on it, died on it, or jumped from the wardrobe on to it I shudder to think, but it is large, uncomfortable and the mattress is made of horsehair. I was wondering recently why so few of my professed friends stayed the night; this horsehair nightmare gave me the answer. To start with the bed was hard, with sharp hairs sticking into my delicate skin and my delicate parts in a dozen places. As the hot summer night moved towards dawn, so the horsehair heated up and as it did so it also sagged under my weight. By dawn the mattress had dropped to such an extent that it was like lying at the bottom of a ditch, encased, and cooking in horsehair.

Despite the night, Corset greeted me with love and adoration in the morning. For the next five hours she slept in my armchair like a baby. Because my favourite armchair was taken, I caught up with sleep on the bean-bag. From the homes of my immediate neighbours there was no sound or sign of movement until well into the afternoon.

'Toys', I was told, 'they are the answer. Get her playing with toys. Then, when you put her in her kennel last thing at night, put the toys and bones in with her and you will never hear another sound'. It sounded like good advice to me, so I gave her a cuddly sheep, monkey and gorilla to savage and maul. In addition I visited the local pet shop to see what else could be purchased. I wondered about a squeaky effigy of Jane Root, the Controller of BBC2 – the woman who will not bring back a proper series of One Man and His Dog, or perhaps a fluffy Rolf Harris. Instead I purchased a wonderful rainbow coloured rat, complete with whiskers and a squeak when bitten.

Corset immediately took to Jane, flinging her about and making her squeak incessantly. It can only be a matter of time before the RSPCA begins a campaign to ban squeaking toys; they clearly encourage puppies and kittens to bite. Perhaps the campaign can be started by St. Paul McCartney? Night fell; the toys and bones went to bed with Corset and immediately the kennel door shut the decibel level of complaint reached new and dizzy heights.

I am glad to say that with perseverance, good understanding and deaf neighbours, after five nights, Corset became quiet and calm, sleeping peacefully with her bone and her rat until the sun was up. She then started a new tactic – her very own dawn chorus – 'it's five o'clock, so get up', was her message. It is odd, Corset wanted to get up at about the same time Euan Blair sometimes gets home, or so we are led to believe. Does this mean that Corset is better behaved than the Prime Minister's son? Of course, if anybody in my village high street is found incapable in the early hours while their parents are away, they are described as being 'latch-key children', but apparently we must not criticise the way family man Tuscany Tony brings up his children. Simply writing this chapter may provoke a complaint to the Press Council, or who knows, Denim Man may even fly off, courtesy of the Queen's Flight, to see a lawyer. I don't care what Tony Blair says about the way I am bringing up Corset. I simply know that she is going to grow up into a charming, well adjusted hound, with better manners and a better life style than many members of the Cabinet.

27

Losing Your Deposit

_____

Hounds we know have a great reputation for courage and bravery. So it came as no surprise to find that Corset too had inherited the bravery gene. One day, with her hackles up, from the back of her neck to the base of the spine, she barked at the rug on the washing line with great ferocity. At the sight of her first horse her decibel level increased several fold and even frightened me; was this, I wondered, the only foxhound in Britain that could not stand horses.

Her cum-uppance came with cows; after counting their legs and dividing by four she decided that there far too many for comfort and ran home. Once in the house her bravery left her altogether. I had left the living room door open; oh, what fun, she climbed the stairs, jumped on the beds, attacked a sheepskin rug and then wanted to return downstairs. This too was beyond Corset; not only was she a hound that hated horses, but she was also a hound with no head for heights. She cried, she howled and she would not go anywhere near the first step; it was much too high.

On rescue I was clearly seen as her great hero. She danced with joy and kindly nipped a section of my midriff with her teeth in appreciation. It was not appreciated by me however, although I was amazed that in my condition there was any spare midriff for her to nip.

Sadly her fear of heights did not last long. Now whenever the living room door is open she is off upstairs. It is all good training of course for a hound because she is hunting. She is not hunting for Jane, the squeaking psychedelic rainbow rat, she tired of that sometime ago; she has found something far more challenging – the lavatory brush. Wherever I hide it, she finds it and she always appears with it triumphantly whenever someone knocks on the door. I suppose it does at least prove that I have a lavatory brush, but I do not want to be presented with it when I am about to eat dinner. Today I am actually going to eat casseroled grey squirrel, peas and mashed potato. I really don't want the lavatory brush to appear as I am tucking into such a delicacy.

Mr. Blair and the RSPCA claim that it is easy to house hounds. I have still failed to wean Corset from my armchair. After every activity it is a race to see who gets to the armchair first. If I win, then she follows immediately afterwards, jumping onto me from two yards. Head first, I can just cope, but sometimes she seems to twist in the air and she arrives tail first. It is frightening; it is like having a mug shot of Robin Cook coming at you with great speed.

The other myth emanating from the RSPCA is that hounds can be easily housetrained. When Corset arrived the days were warm and the doors were open, and after one accident leading to the rug being on the line, all appeared to be well. Then the rain came. The doors were closed and I dropped my guard. As I bounded up to my study in the roof, I did not notice that I stepped into a rather large but soft gift from Corset. It was only when I settled in front of the word processor that my nose started to twitch, rather like a hound finding scent. Yes, I had trailed Corset's deposit all over the house. What had made the deed even worse was the fact that she had done it on my wallet, my father's old wallet, carefully put away on the floor. I was not worried about the money inside, half-a-crown, old money, I was concerned for all the rare moths inside that had been put in grave danger.

But when all the clearing up had been done I was grateful to Corset, for she had reminded me that at the moment there are many other unsavoury deposits that have still not been cleared up. Yes, we have all heard again about the £1m deposited by Formula One. What I would like to hear about is the truth concerning the £1.1m deposited in New Labour's bank account by the animal welfare lobby. Why has Tuscany Tony hung on to that money; and let us hear of all the Labour Party connections that gave that money. Then, how much have Elliot Morley and Tony Banks received over the years? And what precisely are the links, if any, between Tony Blair and Sir Paul McCartney? Thank you Corset, your deposit reminded me that there may be some much larger deposits along the corridors of power.

28

Sacked for Being an English Peasant

———

Oh dear, sacked again, I think I am becoming unemployable. It came suddenly, out of the blue, from the Features Editor of *Country Living*, a woman called 'Diona'. 'I've been thinking long and hard about how we deal with farming issues', she wrote, ' I believe that the public perception on your stance on hunting, rightly or wrongly, is one of support for the pro-hunting lobby. As you know, it is CL's intention not to promote either side in the debate and I feel that it is necessary to appoint an Agriculture and Wildlife Advisor who is not perceived by the general public to be in either camp'.

Strange this, I do not hunt, shoot or fish, but I am guilty of supporting an activity that is not politically correct. *Country Living* has no problem with the fact that I take sides on other issues, openly and unashamedly – I am against the Government's closure of small slaughterhouses; I believe that halal slaughter makes fox hunting look like a Sunday School outing; I am opposed to GM crops being grown outdoors and I would like Britain to pull out of the Common Agricultural Policy and the Common Fisheries Policy. These views are alright apparently; *Country Living*'s big problem is fox hunting.

Well, did *Country Living* have any letters or phone calls of complaint about my stance on hunting? Not one. As Farming Adviser did my views correspond to those of most farmers? A recent survey in *Farmers Weekly* showed 95% of farmers to be in favour of hunting – so it seems I was sacked because of inner M25 political correctness.

My support for hunting is based simply on a number of straightforward issues. As first and foremost a conservationist, I believe, like the great David Bellamy, that hunting, shooting and fishing are good for wildlife. The habitats deliberately left for foxes, pheasants, grouse and salmon are also good for numerous other species – they are good for 'biodiversity'. As a conservationist too I can see the damage done by both foxes and mink to ground nesting birds – some of them rare. Indeed in my view the decision by Scottish Natural Heritage last year, not to support the idea of mink hounds being taken to the Hebrides to help stop the destruction of endangered birds was irresponsible. It was a case of political correctness being put before the needs of conservation.

I support hunting on animal welfare grounds too; to me hunting is the least stressful way of killing foxes – and I have seen foxes shot, snared, trapped and poisoned. The fox is either caught or it gets away; it is as simple as that. If animal welfare is really the issue, what about halal slaughter. What about the way 800,000,000 broiler fowl are killed every year; what about the 75,000,000 birds and animals killed by cats every year; what about the 250,000,000 birds and animals killed by cars every year etc, etc. All these issues seem to concern the abolitionists not at all. And incidentally what has happened to the £1.1m paid to Labour by the Political Animal Lobby? I thought it was the Tories who were accused of sleaze?

Civil liberties come into the equation too. With farming on its knees, rural communities falling apart, development and incomers out of control, the attacks on hunting simply build up more pressures on our embattled and embittered rural communities. In fact what we are seeing is the deliberate cultural cleansing of the British countryside by an urban majority that does not care, and by ego-tripping politicians desperate for free and easy publicity. Indeed I believe that what we are seeing is a form of fascism sweeping through British politics at the moment and fascism loves a scapegoat. The anti-hunting Hitler had the Jews – he regarded saving foxes as far more important than saving Jews. Our loveable MP's regard saving foxes as far more important than urban renewal, the drug epidemic, NHS waiting lists and the rural crisis.

If the environment is really a concern, as it ought to be, what about over-population, de-afforestation, pollution, global

warming, and, yes, the actual survival of the planet. The direction in which we are travelling at the moment is the same as that enjoyed by the dinosaurs.

In this context, I would have thought that *Country Living* would have had the knowledge and honesty to support hunting – instead they have made me another victim of anti-hunting, anti-rural victimisation and discrimination. If I had been a gay activist or a Muslim activist instead of a countryside activist I believe that my job would still be intact. In addition of course, a gay, or a Muslim would be able to turn to the courts for protection and compensation – traditional country people have no such defence mechanism.

The loss of my job with *Country Living* will lose me little sleep however. I have been trying to get more mud and more real people between its covers. I have failed; the magazine is becoming ever more twee and it reads more like an 'Incomers Guide to Our Rural Theme Park'. If you want real life, with the countryside in crisis, forget it.

Sadly the CL discrimination is not the only one I have experienced lately. A year ago I offered the BBC the serialisation rights of my book *The Hunting Gene*. It would now be the most topical series on television. The Controller of BBC 2 Jane Root turned it down – I believe that she is now also trying to oust me from 'One Man and His Dog' – watch this space.

After twenty-two successful books, I could not get a main-stream publisher to take *The Hunting Gene*, so I wiped out my life savings and published it myself. I have already got my money back and the book is just being re-printed. I did send a copy to the Editor of *Country Living*; with hindsight I don't think that was a very clever decision.

29

Hunting the Emperor

———

I am in a state of great excitement; the hunting season is here again. I refer of course to the hunting season for the spectacular purple emperor butterfly. Although it is not my favourite butter-fly, that privileged position is taken by the beautiful but under-rated orange tip, nevertheless the purple emperor is without a doubt the most flamboyant and largest of Britain's butterflies. It almost goes without saying that because it is such a stunning creature it is also one of the most difficult to see and its eating habits can only be described as disgusting. Whereas the average butterfly chooses to dine on the nectar of flowers, wild or tame, the purple emperor's favoured snacks include decaying 'mixy' rabbit, dog droppings and stagnant puddles. Astonishingly for a butterfly, it is also quite aggressive. If disturbed at its favourite resting spot, the very top of a tall oak or ash, it will often chase off the intruder, whether butterfly or even small bird.

The planned hunt for the purple emperor was special. My only sighting of the butterfly was about twelve years ago with 'BB', Denys Watkins-Pitchford, that wonderful writer and illustrator

of childrens' books such as 'The Little Grey Men' and 'Down the Bright Stream', and memorable countryside books and stories such as 'Wild Lone' and 'The Quiet Fields'. He started each book with a woodcut of a cowslip and the words 'The wonder of the world, the beauty and the power, the shapes of things, their colours, lights and shades; these I saw. Look ye also while life lasts'

He successfully introduced the purple emperor to a wood near his Northamptonshire home and once he took me to see it. At the same time he collected some of the tiny green eggs, laid singly on Broad Leaved Sallow. Every year he took the carefully collected eggs home where he hatched caterpillars and butterflies, in a specially built cage in his garden, for further release into his beloved wood. To help him in his search for eggs he was often accompanied by that notorious hedge-laying legend from Derbyshire, Badger Walker.

So within one month of the tenth anniversary of BB's death I went with Badger and Corset back to the wood to see if the purple emperors were still present. Strangely Badger and Corset had similar searching techniques, both being hyperactive and scurrying hither and thither. As we approached the wood along a traditional country track it seemed a good day for butterflies. Knapweed, tufted vetch and teasel were on flower ('on' flower is Cambridgeshire dialect), clearly marking the purple emperor season. There were many butterflies on the wing and feeding – small tortoiseshells, red admirals, small skippers, meadow browns, brimstones and speckled woods. There were numerous gatekeepers too, an attractive little butterfly of sunny hedgerows, glades and yes, gateways. The name is so perfect and descriptive that inevitably some butterfly bores are trying to change it to 'hedge brown' Someone ought to arrange for a PhD study on why so many scientists have no sense of vision, joy or continuity – give me the country name rather than the scientific name any day.

The wood had changed considerably since my last visit. Much oak had been cut down. There is nothing wrong with that in a wood; the trees are the harvest. The trick is to take the harvest without doing too much damage to the wildlife. There were various dead cars and vans too, along a roadway; the minds of those who pollute even some of our most hidden and isolated patches of countryside are totally beyond me.

Badger's green shirt was a most suitable garment for egg searching. It meant that from time to time on the woodland fringe he appeared to disappear completely. Corset also disappeared completely. She learnt that all things coloured green are not grass, or Badger's shirt. She joyfully ran onto what she thought was a green, grassy glade, only to find that it was a carpet of duckweed over the foulest of foul woodland pools. She struggled ashore from her first ever swim wearing a most fetching covering of duckweed. It looked almost as if Badger and Corset were colour co-ordinated; it would have made a wonderful cover for *Country Living*.

The smell resulting from Corset's Jacques Cousteau experience was absolutely appalling, but just right for attracting purple emperors. None came and we trudged back wearily to the car, all that is except Corset,who rolled and romped with her tail and wanted to remain in the wood.

At the old, round toll house where BB once lived Corset continued hunting – ducks, bantams, dogs and biscuits. There we discovered that the purple emperors were still in the wood, but had moved to the other end, where there had been less disturbance. I was really pleased. Not only did it mean that the purple emperors were still present, but it also meant a return trip.

30

Fleeced Again

———

For me the middle of August has become a very special time; this year it was not the glorious 12th , but the glorious 17th , the day of the Vale of Rydal Sheep Dog Trials and Hound Show. It is a true country show, with not a double glazing salesman, or a politician in sight. There were no stalls of Teddy Bears either, and if there had been the hounds and terriers would have had a field day. It is a show about working dogs, with some of the best sheep dogs and their handlers in the country competing for a variety of prizes. The terriers and hounds are working dogs too and they were joined by trail hounds, who during the course of the day set off in pursuit of an aniseed trail; I am expecting the Royal Society for the Protection of Aniseed to be formed next year.

Because the dogs are working dogs, most of the people who attend are working people; farmers, shepherds and Lake District locals with their roots going back several generations – not simply into the latest holiday home. If during the day I received a pound for every time I was asked about the fate of 'One Man and His Dog', I would still be in the beer tent. Sadly the news is not good. After repeatedly being told by the BBC hierarchy that if last year's 'One Man and His Dog' Christmas Special attracted 2 million viewers, the programme as a proper series would be back in business, the BBC has gone back on its word. The programme attracted 2.6 million viewers, yet there is to be only one Christmas Special again. In my view this is an insult to me, the *Daily Telegraph* and to all those thousands of people who wrote to the BBC last year. To add injury to insult, this year one of the most popular parts of the programme, visiting the farms of the competitors, is being removed completely, oh, and of course, for

having the audacity to criticise the mighty BBC, I have been demoted from main presenter – more about this later.

The other organisation to come under repeated attack at Rydal was the National Trust. Like the BBC, from the Lakes it seems to be a London dominated bureaucracy; it does not seem interested in traditional country people, and its words never to seem to match its actions. Last year after visiting Rydal I visited the National Trust. As farm incomes were tumbling, the National Trust was busy putting up rents. As a consequence I was told of various Trust schemes that would be put in place to help its tenant farmers make more money; it was going to market the traditional Herdwick sheep and it was intending to sell the famous Herdwick wool for carpets. If any of this has been done, the farmers of the Lakes have not been told and life is still hard.

Last year, Eric Taylforth, who farms 250 National Trust acres, had his rent put up by 70%, yet this year, despite all the fine words and intentions he has had to burn his wool again. No National Trust scheme to sell wool or meat has appeared although the Wool Board boasted that payment for Herdwick wool had risen by 300%. In fact it went up from 1p a kilo to 4p with the Wool Board charging 5 1/2p a kilo to collect it. When added to the cost of shearing it meant a sizeable loss on each fleece, and so once again Eric has found it cheaper to burn his wool. One company has started up selling rugs made from

Herdwick Wool, but that has nothing to do with the National Trust, and as yet The Woolly Rug Company is not using enough wool to help many farmers.

Through its size and with its outlets the National Trust should be selling more than fudge and calendars, and it should be helping its farmers to market their produce. Apparently one National Trust official has told potential customers that if they want National Trust Herdwick lamb, they can be bought at Cockermouth or Penrith markets. For somebody wanting a lamb chop this is very helpful news; most markets sell many sheep at a time and the lamb chop customer would then have to arrange to have the beasts slaughtered and butchered – and his deep freeze would have to be enormous.

The Lakeland tenants also have very little incentive to improve their lot; at each effort at diversification their rents go up. One tenant was even advised to apply for Family Income Support, so that he could pay more rent. In addition National Trust tenants have been banned from allowing camping on their land. Now all campers, and their money, are being siphoned onto National Trust run sites.

In twenty years, because of the work and responsibilities of hill farming Eric Taylforth has not been away for a holiday – then I spoilt his short time off by talking about the BBC and the National Trust. However his day was not ruined entirely, he was able to see Rock the Lakeland Terrier win its class in the working terrier show, it was of course owned by Mr. Fox.

Next year's Centenary show will be held on August 16th. It is hoped to hold a celebratory dinner and dance on the night of the 15th. If the organisers want to maintain attendances, perhaps the dinner and dance should be held the night after, rather than before.

31

Country Life

———

Corset, my beautiful foxhound is rapidly becoming a cult figure. At last weekend's Burghley Horse Trials she was almost mobbed like a pop star. If this continues then I will have to purchase an ink pad so that she can sign her own autographs. She enjoyed the event enormously, meeting hundreds of people who clearly thought that she is the most beautiful dog in Britain, and also meeting numerous dogs of all shapes and sizes whom she greeted in the usual doggie manner.

In fact she was so well behaved that she only caused me embarrassment twice. Firstly, it is becoming clear that she is the only foxhound in Britain that dislikes horses. That's right, a foxhound that dislikes horses, and I should get her. Her anti-horse mania started when she saw her first police horse; her hackles arose from her neck to her tail; she growled and then she barked furiously; when three appeared I thought I would have to find a vet to give her doggie valium. She even barked at the competitors, which at a horse trials is not the most ideal form of behaviour.

I bought her a squeaky toy to take her mind of it – it was a plastic head and shoulders of a grinning Tony Blair – nothing new there then. When bitten it squeaked, but sadly Corset found the appearance of the thing so unappealing that she would not touch it. The plastic grin matched the real thing perfectly; if only

87

synchronised grinning was in the Sydney Olympics, Tuscany Tony and his lovely lady wife would easily walk away with the gold. Corset even excelled herself by squatting in the middle of the Country Living tent. Readers may remember that I was, until recently, *Country Living*'s Farming and Wildlife Adviser. I was sacked because, although not hunting, shooting or fishing myself, I took on a too high public profile in support of the pro-hunting lobby, according to *Country Living*, or should it be renamed 'Suburban Living'. Consequently, Corset's simple action seemed entirely justified.

Apparently after my sacking became public knowledge *Country Living* was inundated with subscription cancellations. Now I have been flooded with copies of the mass produced letter the Editor of *Country Living* is sending to all those who wrote in complaining and cancelling. Incredibly, she says my 'advisory role was not a job from which it is possible to be sacked'. So my name is removed; my job is taken away and money has stopped, but in the view of the Editor, whose job is words, this does not constitute 'the sack'; Corset obviously has a clearer understanding of English and disagreed.

I was only able to go to Burghley because we had finished harvest. It has been a stop-go harvest, but just in the nick of time all was safely gathered in. It is a sad indictment of what the politicians are doing to Britain's farms that many farmers are wondering whether it is worth the bother of getting the harvest in safely, with cereal prices lower than for twenty years. It simply does not seem worth all the effort. Yet, despite the fact that wheat is only fetching £60 a ton, and malting barley about the same, I have not noticed a fall in the price of biscuits, bread or beer. If only the salaries of MP's were linked to world prices in the same way as wheat – then perhaps they would take the current farming and countryside crisis seriously.

Of course, the Government claims to be taking the needs of the countryside seriously, that is why John 'Two Jags' Prescott recently announced a major new initiative to help farmers. Behold, he announced, jowls wobbling with emotion, that farmers could get a rates reduction if they started up a horse enterprise. I do not know if John Prescott has ever seen a farm or a horse, but shouldn't one of his advisers, or perhaps the Editor of *Country Living*, have told him that there are already two many horsy enterprises in the country, and doesn't he realise that if Labour is successful in banning hunting, then the demand for horses will fall rapidly anyway. Perhaps he knows, but is not saying what is already obvious – Labour's intention to ban hunting will break European law. At the beginning of October, the European Convention on Human Rights (ECHR) becomes incorporated into British law. This protects the personal freedoms and rights of minority interests and it prevents the rule of a majority from becoming oppressive. Any attempt to ban hunting will contravene the ECHR in several places. Famously, the Europhile, Kenneth Clarke boasted that he had not read the Maastricht Treaty, perhaps the Labour Government has not read the ECHR? At last we have something good coming from Europe.

But, despite the falling prices of corn, and the rising egos of politicians, harvest gave me two wonderful experiences. While waiting for the moisture content of the wheat to fall, I walked down to the hay meadow of the CRT. After the first hay crop, regrowth had created a sward of flowering clover and dandelions; then suddenly, in the bright sunlight I glimpsed a flash of sulphur yellow and I immediately whispered 'Clouded Yellow'. I saw another, and then another – there were well over twenty of these wonderful, spectacular butterflies. Some fed on clover and others just seemed to flit from place to place in the strong breeze. The clouded yellow is a migrant from the Mediterranean and its chosen food plant for egg laying is red clover. I have only seen them in two other years and I felt privileged that the CRT meadow should have held such numbers.

The other surprise came at dusk on the evening we finished combining. I took Corset down to the brook meadows with me to check the sheep. All were present and correct and I watered them using my high-tech water pump of a bucket on a piece of string. As I left the field, a shadow, a white shadow floated over us in complete silence. It wheeled round and passed low over Corset as if taking a surprised second look. It was a white owl, flying in summer. A few weeks ago I found some barn owl pellets in an old barn that has not seen owls for more than thirty years. I hope it means that there are resident barn owls in the parish once more, and if there are, I hope they have bred.

I wonder if Two Jags has ever seen a clouded yellow or a barn owl? He probably thinks they are types of gas guzzling cars.

32

Worrying Times

———

It was a beautiful warm day of early autumn and I was late. I had to be in Shropshire by 4pm for the filming of yet another solitary 'One Man and His Dog'. I still had one more job to do before hitting the road, and that was 'check the sheep'. It has been a good summer for them as the damp season has given them abundant grass. They were still in a small grass meadow by the brook and I had opened that up to allow them onto meadows restored to grass by the CRT, as sheep make the best conservationists on new grass. There had been no problems with them all year, and the temptation was to give them a miss and head north, but like every traditional farmer I respect my sheep and felt obliged to check, just in case.

Peculiarly, they were all bunched up in the far corner of the field. I called them and they came at the trot in single file making them easy to count – 'twenty-two, twenty-three, twenty-four'. One was missing and two were behaving in a strange and erratic way: I was concerned. The missing ewe was my one and only Jacob called Palmnut – yes, several of my sheep have names. We were once given a Jacob already called Peanut; her first lamb was born on Palm Sunday and so she was called Palmnut. That too was an unforgettable day; it was the day my father had a stroke and we brought the new born lamb into the house to show him, while we were waiting for the ambulance.

I had no choice, I would have to be late for 'One Man and His Dog'. I collected Mick, one of my oldest friends and part time shepherd when required. We found the old ewe in a dry ditch by the sprawling hedge. She was on her side, dead, with blood on her throat; she had been throttled. We penned the rest of the flock and the full implications of what had happened immediately hit us. Three other sheep – two ewes and a lamb had throat and facial injuries. One was totally traumatised and another was in a dreadful state. She was bleeding from the neck and both her cheeks had been ripped off, leaving raw, gaping wounds.

John the vet came and administered antibiotics. The verdict was simple; the sheep had been attacked by a dog or dogs and this was a straightforward case of dog worrying. My sheep had become part of the statistics which state that in Britain each year, 24,000 sheep are killed or injured by out of control dogs.

A new battery was put onto the electric fence and Mick and Dennis would administer more drugs and check for dogs while I was away. I arrived in Shropshire at ten that night and although the filming went well, and working with Clarissa Dickson-Wright was enjoyable, for the whole four days I felt uneasy.

On my return I was relieved, there had been no more attacks. Sadly the injured lamb died, but the ewe with the dreadful wounds was hanging on. The end came dreadfully, with blowflies. Her wounds suddenly attracted blowflies by the hundred with eggs and maggots in her mouth. We had to treat her and take her to the farm. Should I shoot her? Should the vet come and put her down, or should I give her one more chance? In the morning she was dead. It had taken her a week to die and I felt great anger and great sorrow.

The traumatised sheep was making good progress, but then another attack came at dusk with yet another ewe getting dreadful wounds to the throat. She was down on all fours when I found her, bleeding profusely. I sprayed her throat with antiseptic spray and injected her with antibiotics; it seemed she must die.

Carrying twelve bore shotguns we scoured the fields for dogs but found nothing. I was supposed to go with Corset to demonstrate at the Labour Party Conference. Instead I was moving my sheep to a field a mile away for the sake of safety. Incredibly the newly injured ewe was still alive and I moved her, with the traumatised ewe for company, back to the farm.

Again the injured ewe was a favourite – half Suffolk and half Texel. Her conception was reported in an earlier book several years ago when my neighbour's Texel ram got out and visited my beautiful Suffolk ewes without permission. Remarkably, the injured ewe, despite her terrible injuries is now almost back to full fitness. The effect on me has been almost as bad as on the sheep. Each day I feel on edge and uneasy, and every evening I, or friends, go on anti-dog gun patrol, with our lead aspirin dispensers at the ready. Three uncontrolled dogs have been seen close to the attack field – two Staffordshire Bull Terriers and a white coloured Lurcher/Deerhound, but they were too far away to catch.

Now I have ten acres of grass that needs grazing, but I am reluctant to put my sheep back into danger. Across the brook is a permissive footpath where assorted dogs and their owners walk regularly. On the CRT land we also have dog walkers on permissive footpaths as well as people who do not keep to the paths. In ten years of keeping sheep, this is my first experience of dog worrying and it has been as bad for me as for my sheep. Sadly, with the right to roam high on the political agenda the suffering of livestock and wildlife at the jaws of uncontrolled dogs is set to escalate – I wonder what the 'listening' Government's spin will be this time?

33

Mental Block

So, it has happened – at last a number of farmers have taken a leaf out of the French book and made history. These were no hooligans, agitators or ego-tripping publicity seekers; these were men worried about their farms, their families, their animals and their future. They were men who had been ignored and sidelined by the politicians and who were acting out of desperation; as far as I am concerned they are heroes of the revolution, and that revolution, to save farming, to save the countryside and to save the country way of life is only just beginning.

The last two years of Tuscany Tony's reign has been a nightmare, in which a whole rural minority has been ignored and rural culture has been under attack by a government that claims to safeguard and represent minorities. As this whimpering public school prefect has been telling us how he has listened and how he does care, I have been turning to the *Daily Telegraph* of February 3rd 2000. The headline was stark and simple; after a brief trip to stay with upper-middle class friends in the West Country, Tony Blair showed exactly what he understood about the developing tragedy in rural Britain – 'What country crisis'? Asks Blair – Rural folk ' are better off than city dwellers'. This from the man who now claims that he has been listening. Perhaps he should join an NHS queue and get a hearing aid fitted.

There have been two last straws. One was yet another handout to the Dome; this Government obviously thinks more of spin, hype and White Elephants than it does about the lives of ordinary people. The other was our own John Prescott, the Bernard Manning of British politics. This great international statesman and controller of the British countryside was very put out by the recent blockades in France. He told the French Government that the action was 'unacceptable'. Unfortunately for John Prescott, many British people found the action very acceptable because it showed what can happen if people take action against non-listening, non-caring, dome-headed politicians.

The British action was spontaneous and born out of desperation. What people should realise is that when a group of industrial workers, such as those at Longbridge, are threatened with unemployment, the Government tries to intervene and the media cry crocodile tears. Yet over the last twelve months 22,000 farmers and workers have been forced off the land accompanied by real tears, trauma and debts and the Government has not called on the EU money that is available to alleviate the problem. The 'listening' Mr. Blair and the 'listening' Nick 'Gay Wellies' Brown should actually try to understand what they hear. Mr. Brown's new top civil servant at the Ministry of Agriculture is a Mr. Bender – perhaps he should try bending his Minster's ear a bit more often.

In the year 1990/91 farmers were receiving £122.3 a ton for bread wheat, over the last year they have received £87.1 and the price is still falling. Over the same period everything else has fallen dramatically too; feed wheat from £114.1 to £70.6; malting barley from £130.1 to £77.1; milk from 25p per litre to 15.9p; beef from £1.28 per kilo to 91.3p and eggs from 42.4p per dozen to 28.1p. It is strange that our food and drink prices in the supermarkets have not fallen and it is significant that the incomes of our politicians have not shown a similar reduction. It is easy for those whose incomes bear no relation to world prices and the free market to urge world prices and the free market economy on everyone else.

So the action on petrol was born out of desperation. My only regret is that there was no blockade near me so I could have done my bit, but I fear there will be many more opportunities for this over the next twelve months.

But the most worrying outcome of the direct action was not the reaction of the Government, but the reaction of the National Farmers Union, the organisation that should have been leading the protests with its President, the so far unknighted, Ben Gill, in the front line. Instead the NFU issued a 'Media Release'. As farmers are going broke left, right and centre, their union declared: 'The NFU does not support the fuel blockade and is urging its members not to take part. Whilst we have long campaigned for a reduction in the rate of duty on fuel, we cannot condone actions which inconvenience vast numbers of people and put businesses – including many farming businesses – at risk. Those few farmers who are involved with blockades and other protests are entirely in their personal capacity and, regardless of any position they may hold in the NFU are not there as representatives of the NFU in any way'.

So 'inconvenience' is far more important than financial ruin!

What a union; what support; what a disgrace. Thank goodness the British public had a better grasp of what was going on.

34

Big White Prescott

Oh dear, I simply do not know how to write about this; I have had a major tiff with Corset. The trouble started when I promised the best looking hound in Britain that I would take her to the seaside. Most dogs like the sea and I hoped it would be a wonderful day. I chose Brighton as the venue and by an amazing coincidence I discovered that not only was the Labour Party Conference on at the same time, but our fun loving Deputy Prime Minister would be there as well. To make things even better, various other East Anglians were also planning to go to Brighton and so a wonderful occasion was promised.

With political correctness high up on the Labour Government's agenda, this did pose a problem. Hounds are not politically correct; they literally speak as they find. Sadly as far as New

Labour is concerned, Corset will be labelled as racist. A week before the day trip, I spent the whole day erecting an electric fence, with Corset in attendance. At dusk I returned to check my handiwork. As I approached the three black spools of wire on a post, Corset went absolutely wild – barking and bouncing up on her hind legs with her hackles up. Yes, in the half-light the fence post looked like a figure from one of my childhood story books – I hardly dare say who – I will be brave – it looked like Little Black Sambo – or in today's parlance an Afro-Caribbean – with the top spool looking just like a head and the second spool looking just like hands. Corset was not amused, but gradually I introduced her to the object and she calmed down. I explained to her that our fun day in Brighton would be multi-cultural and she must relax, although she must expect the nice Mr. Prescott not to welcome our country culture.

It did make me wonder if Mr. Prescott had ever looked at the exploits of Little Black Sambo when he was a boy, after all the book contains many pictures. Interestingly the story is only racist in the minds of the professional race relations industry. Little Black Sambo was written and illustrated by a talented lady called Helen Bannerman. In Malawi there were many Scottish missionaries with the surname Bannerman, and there are still many Africans with the surname Sambo; consequently the story is quite straightforward and accurate, unless of course, you live in Islington. Just think of it, if Malawian missionaries had arrived here first and visited Hull, we could now all be reading a children's book called Big White Prescott. I'm sure Corset would love to get her teeth into that.

The other problem with Corset is that she is 'smellist'. She greets people with certain smells like long lost friends and thrusts her nose into all sorts of embarrassing and unexpected places. This too, could be a major problem, as some members of the Cabinet may actually like it.

As the day of the trip approached, Corset became most excited. I explained to her how the nice Mr. Prescott had seen 'contorted' faces, and how he could never have a contorted face himself. Contortions require muscle control; people who resemble 22 stone tubs of lard cannot control muscle. With one day to go, Corset tried to increase her weight like Two Jags. She went into my sister's kitchen unannounced and standing on her hind legs she found three sponge cakes on the table, ready for an old people's party. She ate the lot with gusto and appreciation. As a direct result she learnt several new words and for the first time saw a flying broomstick.

The night before the trip, disaster struck. As my sheep grazed in their meadow next to a permissive footpath, they were attacked by a dog or dogs. I have now had three ewes killed and three savaged – part of the fruits of the Government's 'right to roam'. It meant that the next day, instead of joining the merry Brighton throng, Corset had to help me move my sheep to safer ground, and so I missed a day that we had both been looking forward to.

Later, to avoid total disappointment, I did point out the lovely Mr. Prescott and his wife to Corset, on television. The incredibly black-haired lady was launching a wide-bodied boat that looked the same shape as her husband. With hair like that, it is fortunate she did not fall in; she would have looked just like an oil slick.

35

The Cultural Cleansing of Rural Britain

Today at 2.30 a meeting is being held at Number Ten, described by some as 'a food and farming summit'. Alas it is no such thing. As the countryside crisis intensifies and farm bankruptcies and suicides rocket, the 'summit' is a cynical attempt to get two individuals off the hook – Tony Blair, and the President of the National Farmers Union, Ben Gill. Tony Blair wants to be seen as the listening and caring Prime Minister, when it is quite clear from his famous West Country comment 'there is no crisis in the countryside' that he neither listens to rural Britain nor cares about its future. In his West Country ramble he claimed that rural incomes were doing well, a judgement made by mixing the incomes of land workers with those of countryside incomers and selecting an average. If a bank clerk manipulated figures in the same way, he or she would be accused of fraud.

Ben Gill on the other hand has, with his union, lost the support of many of the people he represents. Farmers are leaving the NFU in droves and many only remain to receive the benefits of the Union's insurance company – NFU Mutual. Gill wants to present himself as the man with access to the Prime Minister. In reality he is the man who has led his members into the cul-de-sac of the Common Agricultural Policy; many followed, but unless brave and radical decisions are made quickly few will emerge still farming.

In saying this I am not being wise after the event. Being both a farmer and Chairman of the Countryside Restoration Trust I have been giving this warning at meetings up and down the country for years, and now these warnings are coming true. When I first gave them I would be immediately ridiculed by the local NFU representative and the meeting would finish in silence. Now when a Committee member of the NFU tries to say the same thing he is shouted down by the rest of the audience.

Both Blair and Gill are terrified that farmers will take to the streets, following the success of the Countryside Alliance's Countryside March, and both want to preserve their European credentials. The meeting itself is farcical. Thirty members of the farming establishment have been invited; no representatives of small farming and family farming organisations have received an invitation and as far as I can ascertain no environmental groups will be present. The meeting will last an hour and carefully selected representatives will be invited to speak for no more than three minutes. Incredibly, the meeting has not been organised by Blair's normal agricultural and enviromental advisers, but by, according to a senior civil servant, 'some of Blair's New Labour, fast-track civil servants with no rural background'. The NFU organiser has been its Director of Policy, urban-man, Ian Gardiner, famous for wanting food produced as 'cheaply and efficiently' as possible. Two years ago he even claimed that there were 'too many farmers'; he regards skylarks as 'environmental goods' and he does not believe in the 'multi-functionality' of farming – which in everyday language, and in his own language, simply means that 'British agriculture exists to supply a market'. So where does that put the environment, slaughterhouses under EU rules, social policy and rural culture in today's discussions?

The simple and obvious truth is that British agriculture and British rural communities and culture are being destroyed by a number of political decisions started under the Conservatives and finished off under Labour. Cereal prices were allowed to fall to world prices because of an agreement between the EU and the World Trade Organisation. The beef industry was ruined by BSE – a situation created by the politicians and eurocrats – and milk was deregulated through European regulations. The results of all these actions have been disastrous and as far as I am aware they were all carried out with the full co-operation of the NFU. Now, if Eastern Europe is admitted to the EU British farming will be totally finished and the environmental damage done by the CAP in Western Europe will be exported to the East. Already Polish milk is being imported at 10p a litre; British dairy farmers cannot produce it for less than 15p. It is alright for Mr. Blair to claim that world prices rule – neither of his incomes as a lawyer, or as a career politician are influenced in any way by world prices or even market prices.

The solutions to farming's problems are simple, and as Chairman of the Countryside Restoration Trust I gave our formula for a living working countryside at the turn of the year. I would like to give it to Mr. Blair and Mr. Gill today but I have not been invited and cannot get an invitation. The countryside demands simple and political action:

1 The whole of the UK should be eligible for inclusion into the arable stewardship scheme, thereby making each subsidy an environmental one.

2 Slaughterhouse closures under absurd EU regulation should be stopped for the sake of animal welfare and farm economics.
3 Development should be stopped in the south and east. Employment should go to the people, not people to employment.
4 Quadruple the council tax on second homes so that more people can live locally.
5 Subsidise rural transport for the sake of rural communities.
6 Reintroduce deficiency payments. When prices for farm goods are high there would be fewer subsidies. When prices are low farmers and farm workers would get a living wage.
7 The Government should sponsor a campaign to buy British food.
8 Village stores should be able to buy food at the same price as the major supermarkets.
9 Re-establish the Milk Marketing Board to bring back sanity and humanity to the dairying industry.
10 Take action against the absurd amount of red tape for every farming activity.
11 A tourist levy should be charged on all visitors to National Parks and the money directed to farming and rural communities.
12 The EU must not be expanded Eastwards without the necessary environmental and economic safeguards for the rural communities and wildlife of both Eastern and Western Europe.

At the moment Mr. Blair seems very worried about the possible loss of 5000 jobs at Longbridge; he seems totally unconcerned at the loss of 22,000 farmers and workers in the last two years alone. Unless drastic action is taken quickly what we are witnessing is not the 'restructuring' of British agriculture, we are seeing the cultural cleansing of rural Britain. Does this mean that we should call our Prime Minister, Herr Slobadan Blair?

36

House Proud Hound

———

Living with Corset has taught me one very important lesson; contrary to the view of the RSPCA, most people in Britain would find it impossible to live with a hound. If a person is house-proud, worries about breakages, reads *Country Living*, has a keen sense of smell, minds if the favourite armchair is always occupied, objects to the house-guest drinking out of the lavatory, hasn't got two hundred and fifty acres at the bottom of the garden, can't cope with the car passenger trying to get into the driver's seat at 70mph and doesn't like the prospect of paws the size of Steve Redgrave's oars trailing mud onto the carpet – then forget the idea of having a hound. I love living with Corset only because I am a peasant, living in a hovel with roughly the same living standards and social aspirations as the average hound. (In fact, while I have been typing this piece, Corset has managed to force her way into the bathroom where she has shredded a sponge effigy of Mr. Blobby and spread the remains of a tablet of soap all over my bedroom floor – pink soap). The only real way in which we differ is that I greet guests with a polite handshake, or gentle kiss on the cheek, if they are not wearing pink socks, whereas Corset greets them with a full and thrusting nasal inspection.

The one person I would like Corset to live with is the dapper and rabidly anti-hunting Labour MP, Tony Banks. Not only would a fortnight with Corset make him look more working class, instead of like a middle-aged male model, but it would also teach him what wonderful dogs foxhounds really are. I say all this because I recently had the dubious privilege of sharing a platform with Tony Banks, on Radio Four's 'Any Questions'.

I have to say that before and after the programme 'Banksie' was quite personable – the East End cheekie-chappie 'know what I mean mate?' But during the programme he went through his usual anti-hunting litany. It is 'cruel', 'barbaric', no different from 'cock-fighting, bull baiting and dog-fighting'. A strange choice these, because as I understand it these three 'fighting sports' were normally associated with towns and they were particularly strong in the East End of London. In any case, equating the 'fighting sports' with hunting, is like saying that people who like boxing (Tony Banks defends it as being part of his urban culture) would have also defended bare-knuckle fighting, duelling at dawn and sending children up chimneys.

After the show 'Banksie' offered me a drink: 'Red wine or white, Robin'? 'Oh', he continued in horror, showing his urbane urban standards, 'we can't have the white, it hasn't been chilled'. He ought to come out into the countryside sometimes, he would see white wine drunk so warm that it steams and I even know people who would drink Chardonnay with mosquito larvae swimming in it.

I am going to send him a copy of *The Hunting Gene* and I am also going to invite him to Cambridgeshire to meet some real country people and to meet Corset. If he accepts I will take him to the field in which Corset was recently involved in her first serious hunt. I took her at dusk to a grass meadow restored by The Countryside Restoration Trust. There were at least ten hares on the eight acres; some grazing and some just watching the world go by. Halfway along the field one of the hares suddenly sat up and sprinted towards Corset at full speed. She stopped ten yards away and sat up as if to say: 'Excuse me. Excuse me. Are you a hound? I am over here'. She looked at Corset; Corset looked at her. The hare jumped in the air and sat down again. Corset set off in hunting mode; the hare set off in a half circle skipping and jumping, as if to say: 'I'm here, please chase me. Come on, you can do better than that'. The hare then ran slowly past me, skipping and jinking at about one third of normal speed, keeping about twenty yards in front of Corset for the entire length of the field. She could have vanished into a hedge at any time. At the end of the field she accelerated away and a humiliated Corset came puffing back to me. Without a doubt, the hare had actually wanted to be chased. It had been an act of great cruelty – cruelty to Corset. What is Tony Banks going to do about that?

37

Cash for Questions? No Cheques for Legislation

Oh dear, my hunting dog is hunting so well that dear Mr. Blair, in his present state of mind, is likely to declare her a 'criminal'. Yes, according to the Queen's Speech, Corset, my lovely, loveable Cambridgeshire foxhound is to be turned into a villain. As Denim Man approaches another election he has remembered the £1.1 million paid to Labour before the last election and he is proposing to thank the donors by outlawing hunting. So with NHS waiting lists getting even longer, globalisation causing the destruction of British industry, crime out of control and the word 'transport' creating a range of reactions from hysterical laughter to suicide, Tony Blair, statesman, father of lovely Leo, husband of gorgeous Cherie, thinks that the most important and relevant piece of legislation is to stop people chasing foxes over muddy fields. What vision, what priorities, what a total hypocrite and prize plonker. From his ham acting at the Despatch Box in the House of Commons he deserves to be given the part of the son-in-law in a remake of 'Till Death Do Us Part'.

To celebrate her elevation to potential criminal and martyr, Corset sent me into a state of ecstasy – she 'spoke' for the very first time. I was simply walking her round a small five acre grass field, Bullock's End, as I do most mornings, when suddenly her nose went down and her tail went up and she was off. As walk turned into run, there came the sweetest sound I have ever heard, a deep throated 'wuff, wuff-wuff'. It was wonderful; that is all there was, but it was still wonderful and whatever it was she was hunting I have absolutely no idea. It might have been a rat, rabbit or even a mouse, but the three wuffs were unforgettable.

They made all the traumas – the drinking out of the lavatory, the theft of my armchair and the squalor of my living room – worthwhile. The physical and emotional cost of turning her into Britain's greatest hunting machine has been enormous, from her very first walk, to the very last. Her first ever walk with me was again around Bullock's End. Then, she was a puppy, small, innocent and looking to me for guidance and protection. I decided to walk to the middle of the field to check a small sycamore tree I had planted. Most conservationists hate sycamores, as being alien invaders. I like sycamores as the quality of the wood is wonderful and the trees flower, attracting thousands of insects, at a vital time for swallows trying to rear their young. Ten yards away from the tree I felt a crunching sensation under my foot; I had trodden in a partridge nest, and needless to say it was a rare English Partridge. I could not believe it.

As our walks grew longer, so we were accompanied by the farmhouse Labrador, Jonah. Oh dear, more bad news for Denim Man, they hunt as a team, making them both potential criminals. Jonah loves the water and is one of the most gifted proponents of the dog paddle that I have ever seen; perhaps he could even make the Senegal Olympic team. He was on one side of the brook, and both Corset and me wanted to join him. Corset, being well mannered, was keen that I should jump the brook first, but it always seemed just too wide. Then I found a stretch that was almost jumpable, but I wanted Corset to jump first to test the landing of very green grass the other side. Would she jump? Her facial expression seemed to be saying: 'After you Robin. After you – I insist'. She would not go first so I jumped. Corset had been very wise; the grass was floating and I sank in up to my waist. On seeing where the solid ground was, Corset immediately jumped across with ease, making it hard for me to climb out, trying to lick me, wagging her tail and wanting to play.

The last walk was today and it very nearly ended in tragedy. I was visiting new land that is being purchased by the Countryside Restoration Trust as an extension to it Lark Rise Farm. I was walking along the bank of the brook, with Corset and Jonah hunting ahead for rats, moorhens and pheasants. Jonah had been in the swirling, rising water several times and Corset had thought about it, but on each occasion had lost her nerve. Rain was falling, wind was blowing and the light was fading. Jonah was in again and swam towards the far bank, under an overhanging hawthorn covered with a tangle of brambles. Corset watched. Suddenly there was silence; I could not see into the gloom between water and tree. Corset looked concerned. Suddenly there were two loud, piercing yelps, a splash and a swirl; one second Jonah's head was there, then it was gone – he was under water. I started to take my Barbour off, but I could not see him and the water was deep. All I could see was brown swirling water and no Jonah. After what seemed like an age his head appeared, but he went under again straight away. I was going to plunge in regardless. Again he came to the surface and inched himself through the current, head just above the water, struggling. Usually Corset greets his landfall with enthusiasm; this time she hung back concerned. I pulled him out exhausted. He was a very lucky dog.

38

One Drip Too Many

Throughout history, whenever there has been trouble, a figure has arrived from nowhere to overcome the problem. So it has been with the floods – as rain, flood and pestilence washed through lowland Britain, so a saviour arrived, as if from Heaven, apparently promising that the rain would stop; the water would cease to rise and flood barriers would be erected. Never, since the days of King Canute had a British statesman shown such a deep understanding of water: if only Tony Blair had decided to become a water engineer instead of Prime Minister and first President of Europe, then I am sure that there would have been no flooding problems in York or Worcester.

For me, there was only one problem with Saint Tony trying to control the weather and calming the people; I actually like floods and flooding and so does Corset. It is also true to say that flood water and not houses should be on flood plains and so I was glad that the Prime Minister kept away from our floods – his arrival would have been one drip too many.

Corset was a bit wary at first when the water came, she could not quite work out how and why some of her favourite bramble patches had become part of a marina. To make it worse for her as she tip-toed around the edges of the water, unsure how to approach this swirling, muddy mass, the farm Labrador, Jonah loved it, jumping into the strongest currents and doing a reasonable impersonation of an overweight otter. Sadly, Jonah is quite mad; the subject for his watery excitement is usually neither pheasant nor fox, but a marooned mouse. I suppose if I bathed more often Corset would have had a greater appreciation of water, but I only bath twice a year, on the longest day and the shortest day. Never mind, my second annual bathnight is approaching rapidly.

Slowly but surely Corset got to grips with the water. Gradually, from jumping every puddle and skirting every flood, it got to jumping into every puddle however small and dirty and running through the edges of every flood at great speed in a great cloud of spray. So happy was she that she wanted to share her joy with everybody and anybody she met; now numerous people have giant wet paw marks on their chests.

Despite her water games, spray and hunting Jonah, Corset still will not swim. One afternoon I took her over a submerged bridge with the water just below welly level. The hound took the wrong line and disappeared from view. She seemed to go a long way down, but before a heroic rescue act was called for she surfaced, her long elegant front legs being anything but elegant as she performed the worst dog paddle in recorded history. Now she approaches submerged bridges with much greater caution; she will cross them carefully; she will still run and jump through the shallow floods, but she will not swim. If only our modern day King Canute would come and bless her I am sure that she would develop the best dog paddle in the world.

One afternoon along a meadow, there seemed to be a familiar figure that I had not seen for almost a summer. She had a dog with her; a little white terrier. They were both enjoying the flooded fields, the warm sunshine and the beautiful light of approaching dusk. Life plays many tricks. It was the woman who, at the time I started to write *The Hunting Gene* was going to be my wife; on the day I sold *The Hunting Gene* for the first time, in February, at Fakenham races, there was a letter waiting for me on my return telling me that she had married somebody else; it started 'Dear, Dear Robin'.

Corset had never met a white terrier before and was not quite sure what to make of this game, water-loving Jack Russell. Owner and dog loved the fields where Hippy had once hunted, swum and played. We walked towards the next field close to a road going over a disused railway line. Corset was happy trotting ahead, sniffing the air for anything interesting – Hippy disappeared. With the amount of rain, rabbits had almost certainly been flooded out of their burrows. I assumed he was rabbiting and that Corset too would soon put her nose down and her tail up to begin her own private hunt. A car came over the bridge at speed. There was a muffled bump; I feared the worst. The car sped on, but another stopped. On the bridge a lady was cradling the little terrier in her arms. He had a gash on his head and blood was coming from his nose; Hippy was already dead. Corset looked worried and concerned.

I dug a small grave under a fine old oak tree and Margaret had tears in her large blue eyes. A familiar figure wearing a cowboy hat approached – the vicar from the next village, an advocate of woodland burials, he was also admiring the floods. He stopped at the sight of two people, a subdued hound, and a terrier placed in a small grave. He said a short prayer about creation, animals and dogs and moved on. A solitary oak leaf, the colour of Corset's muzzle floated down and a tear ran down my cheek. I hope I can keep Corset off the roads.

39

A Child's Tale

The hype says that the way to a child's mind is through story telling; magic, mystery and merchandising are the order of the day. Harry Potter has set a new fashion in motion for children's books, and as reported recently, Artemis Fowl is in hot pursuit and his creator, Eoin Colfer has just concluded a deal that could net him over one million pounds. I have never been a follower of fashion, but I too have just written two children's books, aimed at children between the ages of 6 and 106, and they have absolutely nothing to do with magic, mystery and merchandising. They have very little to do with money either, as I have published them myself and I will be lucky if I break even. The stories are short and simple – *How the Hedgehog Got Its Prickles* and *Why the Rabbit Stamps Its Foot*. The titles explain the aim; they are a cross between The Bible and evolution – God and Charles Darwin. They join *How the Fox Got Its Pointed Nose* and *How the Heron Got Long Legs*. With little imagination I have called the series 'The Quite Right Stories'.

The reason for them is simple. I have enjoyed a life in which wildlife, and once everyday birds, bees and animals have been a very important part. I have watched wildlife living normal lives out in the countryside, but I have also been privileged to share the lives of some who have become pets due to injury, misfortune or simple opportunity. Over the years I have had rabbits, foxes, jack-daws, a tawny owl, a kestrel and even, briefly, two badger cubs. In addition, when small, a niece and nephew kept a hedgehog cub through the winter and gave him the name 'Prickles'. This close-ness to animals has helped to create a love for the countryside, which in turn has developed into an environmental awareness which I would like to share with John Prescott, Secretary of State for the Environment. Sadly he comes from a different, urban back-ground, with a different culture and so he appears unable to understand the problems that confront wildlife and the environ-ment today. In fact Britain is one of the most urbanised societies in Europe and so the gap between town and country, nature and 21st century suburban living is greater than it has ever been before. It is easy to mock, but questionnaires really do show that a majority of children today think that potatoes grow on trees and that milk is manufactured in supermarkets.

One of the great challenges therefore, is how to get children away from their computer games and virtual reality and put them back in touch with nature – reality. It is only an under-standing of nature that will ensure that they have clean air to breathe, water to drink and soil to grow them food. It is only understanding, too, that will create a sense of responsibility towards those creatures which share the planet with us. Consequently, I see simple stories of fantasy and imagination about still common animals as one of the ways to put children in touch again.

Looking back to my childhood, books about wildlife, people and animals were very important and made their mark. I can still remember my mother reading Kipling's *Just So Stories* to me. *How the Elephant Got Its Trunk* was my clear favourite. Indeed a few years ago when I was in South Africa, heading for Botswana, I became genuinely excited as I approached the 'great, grey, green, greasy Limpopo river'. On arrival I was so disappointed; it was dry, through over abstraction of water and I drove over the bed without getting my tyres damp.

Beyond Kipling and Little Black Sambo, other books also made a big impression on me. *The Fifteen Rabbits*, by Felix Salten, the author of *Bambi*, was the first book to make me cry at the demise of a rabbit, and there were two others, a few years later, that also made their mark. Jack London's *White Fang* was a book of immense tension and trauma, and then came Henry Williamson's *Tarka the Otter*. I have lost count of the number of times I have read it since crying my eyes out at the age of fourteen because of the death of Tarka. Two years ago I read a few of my favourite book passages on local radio, Radio Cambridgeshire, and foolishly tried to read of Tarka's demise; it took me all my time to get to the end. I suppose that partly explains my joy at the return of otters to our local little brook in 1993, and it emphasised to me the impact of the written word.

Consequently, it seemed to me that one way to a child's mind is still through words and pictures. It had worked with me and I hoped that it would still work with children from a more urban background – after all, that great fighter for conservation and the countryside, David Bellamy, is the unlikely product of an urban background. I wanted to write a simple story, using the artists of my choice, and so ten years ago I wrote *How the Heron Got Long Legs* and *How the Fox Got a Pointed Nose* and published them myself. They were attractive little books, and amazingly I broke even on their publication, although it was an immense logistical problem getting them into shops.

This year has provided me with the solution. When I decided to publish *The Hunting Gene*, as well as write it, my decision was helped by the fact that Merlin Unwin of Merlin Unwin Books, and grandson of the publisher of Tolkien, offered to get 'The Gene' into the bookshops for me. The gamble worked. The book is now into its second reprint; I have recouped all my money, and a little more, and as a result I have been able to produce *How the Hedgehog Got Its Prickles* and *Why the Rabbit Stamps Its Foot*, with Merlin Unwin again getting them into the shops. Once more I have used artists of my choice – Roger Phillippo has drawn the hedgehogs and John Paley, the rabbits. Roger Phillippo is a glass engraver of great ability and eccentricity and John Paley is a Norfolk artist and cartoonist in popular demand. I do not expect my hedgehogs, rabbits, heron and foxes to make me the money of Harry Potter, but somewhere I hope that imaginations will be stirred and interest will be stimulated in the creatures that share the land with us. All I want is a new Bellamy to be inspired this Christmas; the countryside needs some new fighters and I hope that the 'Quite Right Stories' set them on their way. To start the ball rolling I have sent a set of books to Leo Blair, in the hope that they will inspire in him a greater understanding of country matters than that achieved by his father.

40

Living with a Criminal

This will be a strange Christmas; according to the lovely Mr. Blair and his friends I will be sharing the festive season with a criminal. Yes, with hospital waiting lists getting longer, crime out of control and transport stuck in the sidings, Denim Man has decided that the most important issue in this session of Parliament is the chasing of foxes over muddy fields by people with nothing better to do. So, Corset, my wonderful friend, and the best looking seventy-pound foxhound puppy in Britain will be labelled a criminal.

Corset is guilty of many things, but surely in any sane society a dog chasing foxes ought not to be considered a crime. If it is, then worldwide there is a huge criminal class with four legs and two. Corset chases many things, mice, rats, rabbits and pheasants, all perfectly legally, but apparently if she ever chases a fox, then there are Labour MPs who think that such an event would be totally unacceptable. Halal slaughter is acceptable, but a dog chasing a fox is beyond decency.

All this is bizarre, as Corset has far greater failings than chasing foxes. Her favourite hunt takes place when I fail to close

the living room door. She will sneak upstairs, then, after she has finished drinking out of the lavatory there will be a loud crash as she sees the lavatory brush and jumps on it. Why this should continue to be such a prized quarry I have no idea; it is then hidden in various parts of the house, often to the horror of any unsuspecting visitor.

It is reindeer time again and Alan and Tilly Smith have been stopping off for rest and recuperation as Father Christmas and his reindeer have been travelling from one shopping centre to the next. On checking their bedroom before one flying visit I was horrified. The bedclothes had been heaped into a pile and they were covered with large muddy footprints. I carefully pulled the pillows and duvet away. There in the middle of the bed was a large half eaten bone. A bone on its own would not have been a problem, but a bone already dug up from the garden and then reburied in the middle of the bed while still covered with water-logged clay was a real problem. Never mind the RSPCA says that foxhounds can be 're-housed'; if the RSPCA says this, then it must be true.

At least Corset has not barked at the reindeer – Father Christmas yes, but not the reindeer. The reason is simple, she loves the reindeer, particularly reindeer droppings, which she finds even more appealing than old bones. Then after finding me, she tries to lick me as a sign of appreciation.

As usual the Cairngorm reindeer have been very popular all over the country, all except to one woman in Manchester. Sadly she did not have Corset's appreciation and made a complaint; 'I did not come here to see animals defecating'. Not only did she complain in Manchester, but she also phoned the next venue, Huddersfield, to warn of the impending health hazard. If the present Government hears of this then we can expect more rapid and much needed legislation. Forget global warming, the Parliament Act will be used to push through a Bill forcing Father Christmas to put Rudolph and his friends in nappies. This could open the way for a whole new view of Christmas. They may be white nappies, or festive Christmas scene nappies, Rolf Harris nappies or even Union Jack nappies. Christmas will never be quite the same again.

One little boy visiting the reindeer kindly brought five enormous carrots. Sadly neither reindeer, nor foxhounds, nor foxes eat carrots, if only reindeer could be persuaded to eat them, night navigation would be so much easier and the reindeer would be able to avoid strange ladies in Manchester.

I am a great fan of Father Christmas, and this year he kindly gave me an early present – a record in the charts with a message most appropriate for Corset, 'Who Let the Dogs Out' by Baha Men. It was the anthem of the Barmy Army on England's last cricket tour of the West Indies. My niece was most impressed at this new swinging image; she says too that side-whiskers are again 'cool'. I knew that if I left them long enough I would one day be back at the height of fashion. Corset was not amused at the record and greeted the barking with a burst of her own even worse than that directed at Father Christmas.

For the first time this year Father Christmas was faced with a challenge. One little girl who sat on his lap – oh, sorry, I suppose this will lead to another urgent Government Bill re-classifying little children sitting on Father Christmas's lap as 'child abuse'.

Well, the excited little girl on his lap was a member of his Sunday School class. 'And so you go to Sunday School' came the question. 'And do you like your teacher?' The answer should have been 'No, he's overweight, rude and why are you wearing a dress?' Instead the child replied 'Yes, he's nice and makes me laugh'. Perhaps we ought to have a Government Bill after all.

I am now faced with a problem. What to get Corset for Christmas? By then the reindeer will have gone, so perhaps I could buy her some chocolate coated raisins to see if she spots the difference. I can't give her my armchair, she has already stolen that. Perhaps I should get a doggy seat belt so that she stops trying to sit on my lap as we are travelling along the M11. Mud proof boots for her feet would be welcome, or perhaps an air freshener – for both ends. A portable telephone would be another help in case she is ever arrested by Denim Man's Thought Police. I know – I will give her something completely different. I will give her a delayed present; she can come for a walk with me in London on Sunday March 18th along with several hundred thousand other country people. Then the nice Mr. Blair and his friends can put us all in prison; it would be a wonderful way of manipulating the solved crime figures.

41

An Arresting Tale

————

There are two words that describe the current mood of traditional country people, 'outrage' and 'despair'. With 450 farmers and farmworkers leaving the land each week; with farming suicides heading the league table of desolation; with rural communities falling apart, the Government's bigoted and vicious attack on hunting is the last straw. Yes, it is known that the Bill contains three options; hunting should continue unchanged; it should continue regulated or it should be banned, but it is also known that Tony Blair, and his wife, both favour the third option and Tony likes to get his way.

To country people in the beleaguered Lakes, on Exmoor, in Wales, it is hunting that gives them hope, contact with neighbours and a sense of belonging – as seen and appreciated by members of the Burns Inquiry into Hunting with Dogs. For them the attack on hunting is wounding, malicious and without reason and it is because of my support for these hard working, hard pressed rural communities that I joined thousands of other demonstrators in Trafalgar Square on Wednesday. Our gathering was to coincide with the Second Reading of the Hunting with Dogs Bill, announced in the Queen's Speech. As a non-hunting, farming conservationist I do not have a problem supporting hunting – the conservation, animal welfare, civil liberties arguments have all been won, and confirmed by the Burns Report (nowhere in the report are the words 'cruel' or 'cruelty' used to describe hunting); it is the political argument that is being lost because of political bigotry. As Tony Banks said to me after sparring with me on a recent 'Any Questions': 'Don't worry Robin it's only politics'. Wrong, it is more than politics, it is about people's lives and about the cultural cleansing of the British countryside.

At first the Second Reading was to be held on Monday; it was suddenly switched to Wednesday, it is thought deliberately, to inconvenience protesters. Childish political games learnt at school, university and London politics die hard. I heard about the change by mobile phone, it was a simple message: 'Be there we need you – we need all we can get'. I had several such messages from Norfolk, Devon and even Yorkshire – telephone and e-mails organising a protest march from Trafalgar Square to Parliament Square. Contact with the police was being made, for permission, I was informed; I felt that in a democracy in which a minority is being victimised and persecuted 'permission' was an irrelevance.

When I arrived in Trafalgar Square many hundreds were already assembled and by the time we left it had become four or

five thousand. Incredibly the message manipulators of the BBC (known as News and Current Affairs) quite cynically referred to 'a few hundred demonstrators. Several people had dogs with them; sadly my wonderful foxhound pup Corset stayed at home as she was on heat for the first time. If I had known what was to happen she would have been with me; she could have been arrested too and trailed every male police dog in London to Charing Cross Police Station.

The mood was good humoured; there were chants of 'Tony Blair out', there were whistles and hunting horns. Banners proclaimed: 'Endangered Exmoor'; '£1.1m Blair's Bribe' – a reference to the money paid to the Labour party before the last election by wealthy animal rights groups; there was also 'Man of Straw' which was slightly inaccurate, as Jack Straw appears to be one of the few politicians to have addressed the actual issues.

At first police policy was to break the demonstrators up into small groups and keep them to the pavements. Soon we had merged and had blocked off half of Whitehall as we marched. At Parliament Square too we were herded behind police barriers, off the road, despite the fact that police vans parked in the road had already restricted vehicular access. Because of this I felt that we should fill the road, to take our message closer to the MPs. 'Are any of you coming over the barrier with me'? I asked. Seven or eight agreed and I quickly cleared the barrier and headed for the middle of the road; once there I looked behind me – there were no signs of my colleagues. It was like the Somme again, officers and men; I was Private Baldrick and had left the safety of the trenches and was in no-man's land, alone. Where were the officers? Their names will be remembered. I lay down in the middle of the road, wishing that Corset was with me; an unkind onlooker later said that I would have made a most impressive traffic-hump. Two burly policemen, one white and one black manhandled me to my feet and frog-marched me to a van as the crowd cheered – it created a diversion and part of the road was occupied further along by St. Stephen's Gate. The black officer kept trying to force my left arm up my back; fortunately throwing straw and hay bales about regularly meant that he could not do it. I believe that if a white policeman had behaved in a similar way to a black protester it would have been described as 'excessive force'.

After some time sitting in the van with the Constable periodically saying 'Let me see your hands at all times' – I think he was worried in case I had a ferret down my trousers – I was transferred into a small high security van and taken to the Fort Knox of Charing Cross Police Station. Electronic gates opened and we were in a small courtyard surrounded by high walls. I could see a night in the cells looming. I was taken to the 'Charge Room'. It was only then that I was told officially that I had been arrested, but quite what for nobody seemed to know.

Telephones went and there were signs of problems. Apparently the protesters had by now occupied the whole road outside Parliament and were refusing to move until I was released. Over the airways an officer was asking for my immediate return 'ASAP.' I was then informed by the Duty Officer that I was being 'de-arrested' and would be taken back to Parliament Square.

So by police car I was returned; the crowd cheered again; I thanked them for their support and we dispersed quietly, promising to be back if the politicians continue to ignore and victimise the traditional countryside. The police, on the whole, were polite and pleasant – all agreed, from Constable to Officer, that the country protesters were always the politest and most pleasant seen in London. Interestingly they also said, that they totally disagreed with the Labour Party trying to criminalise a normally peaceful and law abiding section of the community. One said, 'It's a disgrace. They're just picking on you as they see you as an easy target'.

So that is how the Labour Party see the Countryside, as an 'easy target'. As they dispersed members of that target were showing signs of running out of patience. If they do, then the year 2001 could see a year that makes the fuel protests look like a Sunday School tea party. Interestingly too, of course, the Hunting with Dogs Bill is illegal anyway; under European law it is an infringement of minority rights. For once something good might come out of Europe.

42

Christmas Crackers

———

Christmas and the lead up to it can be a very exciting time if you are a hound, particularly, if that is the moment when a star appears in the East and you come into season for the very first time. Hence in the sequence of things, puppyhood drifts into adolescence, or in the case of Corset she moved from puppy to exceptionally pretty young lady. I tried to warn Corset of the dangers that could befall a piece of canine crumpet in her condition and pointed to a couple who claimed that their latest baby was a complete accident – I simply didn't want Corset to end up like Cherie Blair; it would be so embarrassing and very much Old Labour and Old Millennium. If only the Blairs had spent more time in the Body Zone at the Dome and less time drinking Chianti in Tuscany it might never have happened.

One thing is certain; if my beautiful hound is undone by some passing mutt, I shall make sure that the culprit does not benefit from his dirty deed in any way. I certainly will not allow him to pose in front of cameras clutching a mug with the whole litter emblazoned on the side; that would be exploitation of the very worst and cheapest kind.

Just as Corset's first change of life began, I took her to the call-over at Coursing 2000. There the hound was astonished to see a handful of 'animal lovers' shouting obscenities and making threatening gestures, while the police just stood and watched. I wish the antis would try the same tactics outside a halal slaughterhouse in Bedford that I know; I don't know who would get them first – the police or the Kashmiri slaughtermen with their rather long knives. It is strange how the outrage of the antis is very selective.

I took the hound to see the coursing on the last afternoon. It was not a success. She barked at the first hare and then she slipped her collar. I was horrified; I had a sudden vision of the hare being pursued by two greyhounds, Corset, all the assembled male greyhounds with their tongues hanging out, a small, hairy fat man shrieking 'Corset, Corset', the judge on a horse, the antis, the stewards, the police and Uncle Mark Prescott and all. I jumped on her before she realised what she had achieved and went back to the car in a cold sweat.

It was because of this collar-slipping trick that I decided not to take Corset up to Parliament Square to protest at the Second Reading of the Hunting with Dogs Bill. As it turned out, that was a serious mistake. When I moved in to the middle of the road for a 'sit down', in what I thought was a group, I suddenly discovered that I was on my own; I had been deserted by the officer classes. I felt rather exposed – like Private Baldrick who had gone over the top too early. If Corset had been there things would have been different. The two burly policemen would not have dared arrest both of us; if they had, every rampant police dog in London would have chased us all the way to Charing Cross Police Station

Back at home the police were almost needed again; I managed to reverse into Father Christmas's Vauxhall Astra parked in the

drive of the farmhouse. As far as I was concerned Father Christmas should have arrived in his reindeer powered sleigh, not by internal combustion; I could not believe what I had done, nor could Corset who was supposed to be navigating in the passenger seat. The arrival of the Cairngorm reindeer and Father Christmas is supposed to raise money for The Countryside Restoration Trust. This year the privilege cost me £400 – or my 'no claims bonus'.

At least the visitors enjoyed the reindeer; unlike a woman at Wigan. There, the council had advertised the deer as 'flying in at 4.30'. 'Why aren't we seeing the reindeer fly', the woman complained, 'it's a disgrace'.

The day after the arrival of the reindeer Corset was in a state of ecstasy – edible ecstasy, I am glad to say. She had found a cast reindeer antler. She seized it in the middle with her jaws and immediately went mad. After charging around a waterlogged field of winter wheat (very good for the living room carpet) she galloped into Bullocks' End with its long grass. With the antlers curving beautifully over her head she looked exactly like one of Rudolph's young helpers. I suppose it must only be a matter of time before a campaign is mounted to stop the exploitation of animals by Father Christmas.

For her own Christmas I gave Corset two presents, both of which are almost certainly firsts for a foxhound. The Christmas

Eve experience was the one that she found most exciting; I took her through the local car wash. As the brushes and soap came round for a second time she actually sat between me and the steering wheel, becoming a very real Corset. When the weather changed and the frost came I gave her something else, and please – no letters. She sleeps on her own, like all decent young ladies of her age. She sleeps outside too and so she deserved it – yes, quite unashamedly, I gave her a hot-water bottle.

43

Food Glorious Food

———

Over the course of several months the lovely Corset has gained many admirers. She gets stroked, patted, cuddled and receives celebrity treatment. Some people even claim that they too would love to have a foxhound. Wanting a foxhound is a very dangerous dream, and as I have already found out it is also a very expensive one. But just how many of Corset's so called fans are serious in their admiration; to me there is a whiff of hypocrisy in the air. In fact it rather reminds of the last Labour Party Manifesto. In it, Tuscany Tone told us, 'I want, above all, to govern in a way that brings our country together, that unites our nation in facing the tough and dangerous challenges of the new economy and changed society in which we must live. I want a Britain which we all feel part of, in whose future we all have a stake, in which, what I want for my own children I want for yours'. An interesting type of rhetoric and very similar in style to that used by Oswald Mosley, and indeed the old Fuhrer himself. Then of course once Blair was in power he isolated country people and turned Britain into the Disunited Kingdom.

So too the attitude of the Corset lovers all changed in an instant. All I said was 'I am exhausted; I need a break to re-charge my batteries for the fight to come – will you look after Corset for three weeks please'. My youngest sister Rachael was last seen running into the sunset screaming; my oldest sister Mary took on the look of a startled rabbit and went off into the garden and started digging a hole and my brother John pretended not to have heard. Roger the glass engraver who will look after her for odd days, disappeared into his wardrobe whimpering and banging his head and Mick, who delivers books for me gave a short two word reply, the second of which was 'off'.

So much for all those people who claim that foxhounds can be rehoused and so much for the RSPCA which similarly claims that it will rehome thousands in the event of a hunting ban. So, there was only one thing to do; Corset would have to return 'home', to the kennels of the Cambridgeshire Foxhounds for three weeks. Paul Roberts the huntsman was happy to have her back; I was traumatised. Two things worried me. What would Corset be like when I got back; would she still retain anything of what I laughingly call her 'house training' and would she still be willing and ready for the march on March 18th?

The other worry was how would she get on at the kennels? Not only with the change of companions, but also with her change of diet. What would her reaction be to 'fallen flesh' – dead cow or even horse. Corset is not spoilt – well not all that much – but she does eat well. A mixture of assorted biscuits, evil smelling tripe and a Bonio at bedtime. This has turned her into a fine upstanding young lady; bigger than both her mother and her father and beautifully formed. It would be a waste of time entering her for the Peterborough Hound Show; she would win it too easily. But how would she take to raw meat – fallen stock?

She takes to 'fallen food' very quickly and if it will not fall by itself she will help it. At Christmas she whipped a slice of ham off my supper plate faster than I could say 'labour sleaze' and when I went out to get an armful of logs, by the time I got back she had eaten virtually a box of mincepies; to make it worse what she hadn't eaten she had kindly trodden into the carpet.

She tried chocolates too; they were a total waste of time as they didn't even touch the sides. Of course she eats other things as well. The worst delicacy she found on the brook bank during late summer. Our neighbour, for some inexplicable reason cuts his brook bank. Why is a mystery; you can't grow anything commercial on the brook bank and uncut it provides much excellent cover for an assortment of wildlife. Anyway, some sad little animal – a rat, a rare water vole, an otter cub, or something got flail mowed. By the time Corset found the feast it was dripping with maggots. It was a disgusting sight; Corset chomping and dribbling with delight; maggots falling from her mouth and my stomach threatening to leave by itself. I suppose she might have found it extremely sensuous and erotic , all those maggots running in and out of her teeth and round her gums, but it was not a pretty sight.

More recently too I was stopped in my tracks. There staring at me from a still steaming Corset deposit was an unmistakable eye. It was dreadful. What had she eaten? It just stared at me accusingly. I had never seen such a thing before, despite gazing into countless deposits of otter and fox. I poked the pile nervously and the answer came immediately. Corset had eaten 'Woody', my tame ash log with two plastic eyes attached to make a face. What a clever woodman's wheeze and what a sticky end. The next day my worry was ended for good: Jonah and Corset found the whole leg of a recent Muntjac road casualty. Yes, after all, she loves fallen stock very much thank you. She also makes a good job of burying the bones, and Jonah is equally good at digging them up again.

44

A Breath of Fresh Air

Life plays many mean tricks and I have just experienced another one. I was supposed to go away to Kenya, to recharge batteries ready for the run up to the March march. Instead I stayed here in dark damp Cambridgeshire, wheezing, coughing and dropping antibiotics as if they were Smarties with the Doctor saying; 'You are going nowhere'. Corset could not believe it; her daily route march turned into a hundred yard stagger and she had never heard so many strange noises coming from one set of lungs. A few months ago I was asked why I didn't belong to the Asthma Society; I think Corset now knows the answer. The meetings must be terrible with all those wheezings and bronchial orchestrations. There can only be one noisier society – The Irritable Bowel Syndrome Society – (there is one I believe) and the Annual Meetings must be a nightmare with periodic explosions and automatic punctuation. I hope they only meet in the summer so that they can have the windows open.

However, my fretting about Corset's diet was justified, as although I stayed here in murky Britain, she still made her first journey back to the Cambridgeshire Hunt kennels, simply to give me a week's break; puppy walking can be very strenuous. So one sad morning I carted her back to her official home and gave her to Paul and Debbie. She was put in with the other huge puppies and female misfits and I turned for home feeling guilty. It is always sad leaving animals behind or giving them away; or at least most people find it sad.

I wonder how those well-known animal lovers Tony and Cherie Blair felt when they got rid of Humphrey, the Cabinet Office cat? Strangely for people who claim to be so much in love with animals and concerned for their welfare, Denim Man and his squaw are reported to have kicked out the cat almost as soon as they moved into Number Ten. The official story is that Humphrey had kidney trouble and so the cat was moved on for its own good. I wonder if after thirty years we will ever find out the truth. We will probably hear that the Blairs simply hated cats and had the beast thrown out because its claws were sharper than Cherie's. Alas it is doubtful that we will ever know; all we do know is that for a cat in supposedly poor health, it is apparently still alive and living a peaceful and joyful retirement in South London.

I worry about the Blair attitude to animals and the countryside. Because of this I sent copies of my four children's' stories to dear little Leo Blair just before Christmas. I told him I hoped they would give him a better understanding of the countryside than his father. I also wished him and his family a very happy Christmas, although thousands of country families would be having a most miserable Christmas. An extraordinary letter came back from Number Ten. It said ' I am writing on behalf of Mrs. Blair to thank you very much for your recent letter and books addressed to Leo. Mrs. Blair has taken note of your comments. I regret, however, that as a private unelected citizen, she has no powers to intervene in matters of this kind'. I was astonished, as it seems to me that this 'private, unelected citizen' has rather a lot to say on public affairs, rather in the same mould as the appalling Mrs. Clinton. Because of this I wrote back asking if the letter was true, as I had been reliably informed that the lovely Cherie had condemned fox hunting at a recent Islington type dinner party. Another load of nonsense came back: 'I am sorry that you were dissatisfied with the reply to your first letter to Leo. Unfortunately Mrs. Blair's office simply does not have the resources to send out individual replies to the hundreds of letters she receives every week'. I wouldn't mind betting that if I had written enquiring about the health of Humphrey the cat, Mrs. Blair's office would have found the time and money to tell me that it was getting on fine. Interestingly, Nigel Housden , a photographer friend tried to photograph the wretched cat recently – he was refused permission. Under New Labour spin that probably means it was run over by a bus two years ago.

Corset enjoyed her stay away and I need not have worried about her change of diet. On the day I picked her up she had been feasting on a dead donkey and her breath gave new meaning to the word 'halitosis'. That evening I had a management meeting of the Countryside Restoration Trust in my living room. Corset slept soundly throughout. But with Bonios meeting dead donkey it meant she did other things throughout. With candles burning, doors and windows open, we only just managed to survive. Perhaps it is Corset who should become a member of the Irritable Bowel Syndrome Society.

45

Rural Blight Paper

———

This is not meant to be a trick question, but apart from the fact that I have done a proper job – in fact several – and he never has, what is the difference between me and Tony Blair? The answer is simple; he is surrounded by policemen and apart from the London variety who seem very keen to put me in jail, I have forgotten what they look like. I did briefly see one in the doctor's surgery the other day, but I was told that the yellow glow was his jacket and not his medical condition.

I do not blame my local policeman for his virtual disappearance; his 'beat' covers eleven villages and so he has no time for 'preventitive patrol work' which was the key to the success of the old village bobby. It is remarkable how our crime 'experts' have not only got rid of the old village policeman, but they have also god rid of their police houses too, thus ensuring that a return to sanity and good crime prevention is impossible.

The fact that rural crime is out of control and that there are no policemen made the recent Rural White Paper a total waste of paper. The other day I had a de-humidifier stolen from one of our buildings; I suppose it is now in a didecoy caravan in Bedfordshire or Hertfordshire. Never mind, just in case the theft left me traumatised I have received a comforting letter from 'Victim Support' and who knows, in the next post they might even send me a box of scented tissues.

The other afternoon I met four charming criminals – didecoys again, illegally coursing hares on CRT land. I let them know in simple English what I thought of them and rather suprisingly my nose and teeth remain intact. What buffoons such as Tony Banks don't realise is that illegal hare coursers are already virtually ignored by the police; they are often violent, do nothing to conserve hares and their aim is to kill the hare. Coursing which is currently legal involves hare conservation and one in seven hares escape, as the aim is to see two dogs run against each other. Presumably if this is made illegal anybody running two dogs will be arrested; hare conservation will stop and the hare population will either be shot or left to the already illegal coursers. It seems to me that the extinction of the brown hare would be rather an own goal for pigeon lovers like Banks – but who knows? Perhaps the welfare of wildlife is not his driving force?

The most amusing section of the Rural White Paper concerns the government's desire to turn post offices into 'one stop shops'. Dear Messrs. Blair and Prescott want village post offices to act as banks, taking in money for local businesses – all this without giving post offices any additional protection and with village policemen unable to carry out preventitive patrols. Four appreciative customers took advantage of this situation in my local shop cum post office the other day. They wore balaclava helmets and wielded baseball bats and an iron bar. How much money they took I have no idea, but they terrified our sub post-master and his wife, both hard working and well-loved members of the community, but the 'one-stop-shop' principle left them vulnerable and at risk. Astonishingly they were then responsible for the replacement of the smashed fittings, as for some reason the Post Office is not responsible for supplying and fitting reinforced glass protection. I hope that the incident will not deter our sub-post-master; in the past, some local post offices visited by such charming customers have simply given up. I am glad that I was not in the post office at the time of the raid, as I almost certainly would have done something stupid. As a consequence I would now either be writing this diary from a hospital bed, or I would be in a prison cell charged with assaulting a didecoy with a tin of grapefruit or half a pound of Stilton. If the robbers return, perhaps they could catch the free bus to Tesco, which disgustingly stops outside the village shop several times a week, and try their luck there.

But there is still one other theft currently taking place in the village, and it involves a whole building. Yes – the Diocese of Ely is selling the village vicarage. As far as I am concerned not only is it a theft but it is also an example of spiritual vandalism, and the local Parochial Church Council appears to have been mugged by the Bishop of Ely and his merry band of cash-flow Canons. The vicarage stands at the heart of the village next to the church, the Hoops, the Village Hall and the school. It forms part of a conservation area and has been the social centre of the village for generations. Now with a new vicar, and extra parishes, the vicarage is to be sold and the vicar is to live elsewhere, despite legacies of land and money which the Diocese of Ely have accepted, which were supposed to guarantee the future of both a vicar and the vicarage in the village.

The vicar is now to live in the village of Coton which is difficult to get at because of the network of roads and motorways on the outskirts of Cambridge. The Coton Rectory already has a tenant on a low rent, so the Diocese has bought the village shop as the new Rectory, thus ensuring the closure of another village asset, and demonstrating both mismanagement and insensitivity in spectacular fashion.

It is a sorry tale, but it shows how and why the Church of England has lost the spiritual and community plot. Sadly spirituality and its pastoral role seem to have been replaced by secular and commercial considerations. In fact to some people the Church of England is beginning to look like a cassocked branch of Bidwells or Savills. Like our poor village policeman the new Bishop of Ely, who seems a very nice man, has 310 parishes under his jurisdiction. Perhaps one way out would be to turn the vicarage into the new police house, complete with padded cells for post office raiders and illegal hare coursers. It could be centrally heated by burning unread copies of the Rural White Paper.

46

No Effing Use

———

For a long time there have been a number of myths circulating among members of the farming community. That farming's problems are being caused by the strength of the pound; that we have to be more competitive; that salvation is to be found in the Euro and in the Common Agricultural Policy. The mythmakers themselves are to be found in large overpaid herds in the offices of the MAFFIA and the NFU. The truth is that the plight of farming has been caused quite cynically by a number of political decisions, ordered by Brussels and obediently implemented by first the Tories and now New Labour – as far as agricultural policies are concerned there is not a scrap of difference between either of them. First it was cereals on world markets in 1992; then it was the BSE fiasco (helped by changed rendering rules nodded through by Brussels with added organo-phosphate chemicals to get rid of the warble fly – nicely evaded in the recent BSE Report); then it was the deregulation of milk with the forced break up of the excellent Milk Marketing Board. What all this achieved was a decline of 90% in farm incomes and 450 farmers a week going out of business; all with the apparent support of the NFU.

Now sugarbeet is set to go the same way with Brussels, after carefully building up a European sugar industry and encouraging farmers to invest in sugar, now pulling the plug by allowing in millions of tons of third world sugar at rock bottom prices meaning that over the next two years, thousands of British sugar beet farmers will be swelling the 24,000 farmers and farm workers leaving the land annually. Such devastation of lives and communities make the 2000 jobs to be lost at Vauxhall's Luton car plant look like chicken feed, yet it appears that it is only the car workers who attract the sympathy and the attention of the politicians and the BBC.

Interestingly of course, sugar cane production is one of the worst crops possible for the third world. Monoculture cane breaks down soil structure; it sets in place a dependency on an unsustainable cash crop and because of the coastal locations of most of the sugar cane growing areas of the world it is responsible for much maritime pollution from fertilisers and chemical sprays. Consequently the new policy is both an EU social and environmental own goal.

It is ironic that in the New Year's Honours List the NFU's Deputy Director General, Ian Gardiner was awarded an OBE for 'services to agriculture'. From where I stand his main service seems to have been one of total support for all the political actions that are killing farming and our rural culture. Never mind; next year it will be the turn of the NFU's President Ben Gill to get his long awaited knighthood.

Regardless of all this, the Countryside Restoration Trust will continue to plough its lonely furrow for both environmentally friendly and profitable farming. We have again invited the Secretary of State for Agriculture to visit our Cambridgeshire project. Needless to say he has once more turned down our invitation. He really has become the worst Minister of Agriculture that I can remember. He appears to have become little more than an errand boy flitting between Brussels and the spin-doctors of Number Ten, with occasional stage-managed forays to see the still Mr. Gill and Mr. Gardiner OBE. He is evidently reluctant to see real farming and country people.

Fortunately a nice lady living near Bath, Janet Clarke can see clearly what is happening to farming and the countryside. She has sent a year's membership of the CRT to little Leo Blair, hoping that it will eventually help him to see the countryside in a much clearer light than his father. To help in the process of educating Leo I also sent him a set of my children's books.

Despite all this, the fight for farming, the countryside and freedom must carry on. Tonight, I take my contribution to the Stadium of Light in Sunderland where I shall be speaking at a dinner in support of Sunderland greengrocer and criminal Steve Thorburn. His heinous crime is that of selling a 'pound' of bananas – in Britain, 'home of the free'. Yes, in Blair's Britain it can be a crime to sell produce by the pound. Forget violence, burglary and mugging, the City Trading Standards Officer of Sunderland wants to criminalise a greengrocer for selling bananas – what a sad man. The great Christopher Booker is also speaking and a certain Mr. Poole is going to sing – almost certainly contravening several European noise directives. I hope to end the evening by becoming a criminal myself; I shall sell a pound of apples. I wonder if the lovely Cherie Blair would like to defend me?

* The pound of apples were sold for £100
** Later Steve Thorburn was found 'guilty' at a Sunderland court.

47

Disappearing

I still live in the village in which I was born, next door to the house in which I was born. In my early years the village did not change. It was a warm place in which antiquity, continuity and security created a community. Communities cannot be created as modern day planners, architects, politicians and social manipulators suggest. My village grew because of the land; the Saxons called it 'the clearing where barley is grown' and barley is still grown here despite our present generations of uncaring politicians who do not seem to like farming or country people, yet alone understand them.

For years nothing seemed to change. The faces, the places and the rhythms of farming and the seasons remained the same. But change did come, slowly at first, with fresh faces replacing old, and new houses built along the High Street and on the site of a small spinney, with the trees being felled just as the rooks were trying to bring up their young. Now change has accelerated to an absurd level and the village has become suburbia surrounded by countryside with the extended family being replaced by strangers living in a dormitory.

Gradually the old villagers gave up. They moved away, died, or simply disappeared, but always one face remained; knowledgeable, faithful and forthright. She stood for everything that is good about a village, but sadly, Ethel too has gone. She was the last of my parent's generation and we buried her in the churchyard where various members of her family went before her. The sun was warm, a robin sang and the organ of the parish church played Jerusalem as she was carried out to her last resting place.

Hers was a long, happy, but hard life. She left school early to go into service and then married Fred, a boy from the village. She had to get married; the need was more understandable in those days with no television sets and an abundance of hay fields. When I first walked the quarter of a mile to school or chapel she lived in an ancient thatched cottage made of wattle and daub. How it stood up I do not know and soon the family moved into a council house close to one of the village pumps.

Fred worked for the local squire across the road in the big house – a grand and pretentious Victorian building now turned into offices, making them even grander and more pretentious. Fred always wore a cap, jacket and tie; Ethel was always smartly dressed, speaking with a genuine Cambridgeshire accent which she retained until the end. Seeing Fred and the squire side by side, a stranger would assume Fred to be the squire. Mr. Holben was a gentleman and a landowner and he was also extremely tight. He wore his clothes until they fell apart, he rarely shaved, and if he saw the coal cart go by he would retrace its route, picking up any lumps of coal that had fallen off.

He had no need for his frugal way of life, but he had turned the lifestyle of Scrooge into an art form. He once paid the blacksmith in sticks of rhubarb and bought a 'load' of hay off my grandfather. He and his men loaded the cart themselves and it took six horses to pull the cart from the field. But despite his meanness, he was a collector of birds' eggs of international repute, and parts of his collection are still to be found in museums at Tring and Baldock. He might have counted his pennies at home, but he spent freely throughout the world, travelling to the most inaccessible places to collect eggs, and Fred travelled with him.

Ethel remained at home looking after her son and her nephew. The home was spotless, the kettle was always on and she lived a busy life. She went to church or chapel, depending on which man of God happened to be in favour, and she was a stalwart of the Women's Institute and the Mothers' Union. On reaching 60 the Over Sixties became part of her domain and she busied herself organising and playing a full part in village life. At church she sang all the old fashioned hymns without looking at the words in the hymn book and at the WI she sang Jerusalem with gusto and pride.

As a working class, Old Labour President of the WI she was not put off by the accentless middle class chutney-makers from the new estates – they cracked their jaws, she spoke her mind and it was a wonderful display of village democracy and unity.

Her power base never extended to the Parish Council: 'I haven't got time for that', she always said. She hadn't either; she was too busy doing everything else. Instead she took annual revenge on what she saw as the follies of the Parish Council. Every year I would sit eagerly awaiting those wonderful words at the Annual Parish Meeting: 'Any other business'. There would be a pause, then Ethel would start: 'Mr. Chairman . . .'

Sometimes it was the village ponds, the smell of 'muck spreading', horses on the pavement, 'why has the parish council done this', 'why has the parish council not done that'. It was entertaining stuff and sadly Any Other Business will never be the same again.

Gradually her friends and relations went on before her and she felt isolated. But her spirit remained high. Every Wednesday morning at coffee time she visited my sister at the farmhouse to get a dozen eggs and just three weeks ago she was there again. It had become a weekly entertainment to talk about old times, new times and put the world to rights. Sometimes she brought me lemon curd tarts, simply because I liked her lemon curd tarts. At our last coffee break at the farmhouse, the visiting thatcher joined us on the lawn. We drank, we laughed, the world was put to rights in record time and we all said 'See you next week'. Sadly next week never came.

48

Very Retiring

In April my brother has decided to pack up farming. There were 24,000 farmers and workers who left the land last year; there will be another 24,000 this year and the figure could be even larger next year. He has simply had enough; falling prices, a deaf and hostile government and a growing nightmare of red tape has caused him to call it a day. Consequently our small family farm will cease to be a partnership and I will have to try and run it myself. The cereals will not be a problem as the CRT's tenant farmer will be able to cope with the extra acreage, but the cattle pose a real difficulty. My writing takes me away from the farm at regular intervals, but animals require attention 365 days a year.

I would hate our beef cows to leave the farm as we have grazing meadows that have been grass for as long as anybody can remember, but the growing burden of red-tape surrounding livestock also creates a massive problem of time and interpretation. There are cattle passports, movement records, TB and brucillosis tests and in addition each new calf has to be 'ear tagged', with incredibly, two tags – not two Jags. To complete the tagging, while keeping an eye on the agitated mother, requires three hands and four feet. It is odd how Health and Safety Officials are quite happy for farmers to risk life and limb when implementing MAFF's mad rules. It would be better if those officials that made the rules had to put them into practice.

The increase in red tape has grown from Mad Cow Disease; the only trouble is that not one of our cattle has ever had BSE and not one of our cattle will ever get BSE. The stock has been on the farm for generations; the bulk of their food is grass, hay and straw grown on the farm and our high protein supplement that we feed in winter, is grown and ground on the farm. Consequently our cattle have more chance of playing football for England than they have of getting BSE yet we are still confronted by this growing tangle of bureaucracy.

Despite this, like thousands of other livestock farmers through-out the country, we have suffered as a direct result of BSE. Through no fault of our own, the media induced scares concerning BSE and the political incompetence surrounding it has meant that we too have experienced a mixture of plummeting prices and rocketing red tape. Sadly the recently published report on the BSE crisis by Lord Phillips does nothing to help us or compensate us. It is a strange situation; those families who have tragically suffered from CJD are to compensated for their trauma and anxiety, but all those farmers and butchers who have had their businesses ruined cannot get compensation for the trauma, anxiety and loss of income that they have suffered and are still suffering.

Interestingly Lord Phillips skates over one important area of both the controversy and the crisis. I knew he would and so I did not bother to give evidence to the Inquiry. In my view one of the key elements in the BSE story is the way in which MAFF instructed all cattle farmers in the eighties to use organo-phosphates to wipe out the warble fly. We had to use it on our cattle, without knowing the possible consequences for them or ourselves. Organo-phosphates affect the central nervous system and it is my belief that the use of these toxic chemicals exposed certain cattle to the risk of contracting BSE. In his Report, his Lordship simply says that organo-phosphates could have 'increased the susceptibility of cattle to BSE'. One thing is certain, there will be no quango demanding research into the organo-phosphate link. If proved, the claims for compensation from everyone affected by BSE would bankrupt the Government. Petrol duty – Tony Blair's liquid poll tax – would have to be increased still further to pay the bill.

In some ways too, the Government's decision to pay compensation to families affected by CJD is strange. There is far more direct evidence linking organo-phosphates with the breakdown in health of some livestock farmers (and Gulf War veterans), yet the government repeatedly refuses to recognise their plight or offer them compensation. Similarly, the media, particularly the BBC, continues to produce scare stories about BSE, while ignoring organo-phosphates. Indeed the BBC has almost become obsessive in its search for a massive BSE epidemic. A few weeks ago tonsils were going to indicate a massive increase in BSE and current affairs programmes became almost delirious in anticipation. When no signs of developing BSE were found in 20,000 tonsils the result from earnest BBC pundits was to demand even greater numbers of tonsils to investigate.

Hysteria is now turning to sheep. Despite the fact that BSE has never been found in normally reared sheep and despite Lord Phillips discounting any link between scrapie and BSE, various BBC programmes and the Food Standards Agency – which ought to be called the Food Scares Quango – are calling for the whole British sheep flock to be screened for BSE. It is madness; British sheep are almost certainly among the healthiest and best kept in the world. Even so, the mad Mafia of MAFF is now saying that all sheep must be ear-tagged with identification numbers next year meaning more red tape and more physical hard work. The Government keeps telling farmers it will cut red tape, but here it is piling yet more on. I have had enough; I am not going to ear tag my sheep as it is both cruel and unnecessary.

At the Royal Show earlier in the year the Shadow Secretary of State for Agriculture, Tim Yeo, told me that if re-elected the Tories would cut red tape for farmers. Taking him at his word I have told him that I am not going to ear tag my sheep and have asked for Tory support. So far he has replied only to say that he will be discussing the issue with his colleagues – the discussion seems to be taking a very long time. Perhaps a good dose of organo-phosphates sheep dip or warble fly killer would hurry the process along?

49

Shambles

The chances of our cattle and sheep catching foot and mouth disease are remote, yet like every livestock farm in Britain we worry, just in case our animals become unlucky and our farm becomes yet another statistic. I would hate to lose our animals; cattle have been on the farm for as long as anybody remember. Although my brother is about to give up farming and I will be carrying on the farm by myself I still want to keep the animals. How I will manage, with my writing commitments, while still running the CRT I have not quite worked out, but I am determined to keep them.

If it were up to me, the concern about the health of the animals would stop tomorrow. I would have them all vaccinated. As I understand it, of the seven or so types of foot and mouth that cause most of the problems, the Veterinary Investigations Centre at Pirbright have half a million doses of five of them, and so if vaccinations had been used after the first outbreak, the present foot and mouth epidemic would have already been contained and farmers could sleep peacefully in their beds.

The tragedy is that the current medieval policy of killing all animals on farms where an outbreak occurs, is carried out entirely for commercial reasons; animal welfare actually takes second place. This is very odd, particularly as the present government claims to seek the high moral ground on all issues of animal welfare. Hence the fate of 17,000 foxes is very high on the political agenda, but hundreds of thousands of cattle, pigs and sheep appear to demand an entirely different set of values. The situation for slimy, scaly haddock is even worse. Around Shetland at the moment millions of haddock are being tipped dead into the sea as our fishermen have no quotas for them under the Common Fisheries Policy. It is a scandal, but nobody seems to care. Ironically the Minister in charge of this man-made ecological disaster is Elliot Morley, another politician who reaches for the tissues at the mention of fox hunting. In the past he has received payments for his office and research staff from anti-hunting organisations. He refuses to tell me how much and so I can only assume the total came to many thousands of pounds. Isn't it odd how some politicians want to reduce farming subsidies but they will not tell us the actual amount of the subsidies they have received?

In fact I have been unfair. The act of killing animals with foot and mouth disease cannot be called 'medieval'. They were more enlightened in medieval times. Throughout history both foot and mouth disease and rabies have arrived in Britain from abroad. The diseases have always died out naturally, as conditions clearly do not suit them and they do not become endemic. When foot and mouth was recognised, the affected animals were taken to an isolated field on the farm or in the parish until they had recovered. Most of them did recover as foot and mouth is a short term condition. It is highly contagious but only five percent of animals' die and most make a complete recovery.

Because of this historical evidence, the scaremongering from MAFF and the industrial farming lobby, about foot and mouth becoming 'endemic' is nonsense. The tragedy is that MAFF and the politicians are plugged into an unfortunate system and will not review it. There seems to be a culture in government which makes it impossible for a politician or a bureaucrat to admit to error.

When foot and mouth breaks out a ring of vaccination would totally isolate and eradicate the disease, without the need, in my view, of further vaccination. But vaccination is required for other reasons as well. In this country we have one of the best collections of rare farm breeds in the world. All over the country there are high quality herds of cattle, sheep and pigs. Their pedigrees go back many generations and numerous breeders and farmers are now realising that some of the traditional breeds can also be highly profitable. Customers are becoming more discerning and they are beginning to appreciate that quality is more important than quantity and supermarket cheapness. It is a mystery why 'cheapness' is the siren call of the supermarkets. I am sure that the Directors of Tesco don't all drive Ladas and have lino on their living room floors.

Vaccinating our rare traditional Hereford and Shorthorn cattle, our Gloucester Old Spot pigs and our Dorset Horn sheep would not only alleviate a great amount of countrywide anxiety, but it would also be safeguarding an important national asset. This is the situation too at a number of our zoos where internationally important herds of endangered cloven-hoofed animals have been built up over many years. Only two years ago I had the good fortune to visit Howletts in Kent, with the late John Aspinall. There he had the largest captive-breeding herd of Bongo, that rare African forest antelope, in the world. Not only is it irresponsible not to vaccinate such animals against foot and mouth; it is criminal for the Government to outlaw vaccination.

Never mind; some good may come out of the foot and mouth tragedy. Both Tony Blair and Nick Brown are now talking about 'sustainable' agriculture. Funny that; the CRT has been talking about responsible and sustainable agriculture of seven years. We have asked both politicians to visit us to see what we are doing. So far they have shown not the slightest bit of interest. Perhaps they need an honesty vaccination, or better still a common sense transplant?

50

Sacked Again – Again

As the countryside sinks into bankruptcy and despair, most of my writing is taken up with defending our rural culture and heritage. What should be my spare time is absorbed by travelling from one end of the country to the other speaking to, and encouraging farmers, conservation groups, hunt supporters and, of course, Women's Institutes. In the last few months I must have addressed several thousand people. My motives are simple; I fear for the long term future of the countryside which I love. I fear for its people, its wildlife and its traditions. Now for my trouble I have been rewarded by the BBC with the sack – I have been sacked from 'One Man and His Dog'. After fighting, alongside thousands of outraged readers to save the programme, I have been told 'we have decided not to ask you to be involved in One Man and His Dog 2001'. To use a phrase much loved by the BBC – I have been 'socially excluded'.

The telephone message, just before the letter was interesting; the BBC's Creative Director said: 'We do not like your attitude towards the programme and your other activities'. 'My other activities'? Strange that; I thought the BBC stood for free speech and freedom of action. Now I have to confess that I have great trouble with BBC telephones. Before the filming of the last 'One Man and His Dog Special', I foolishly imagined that I heard the producer say over the telephone: 'I'm afraid you are being moved sideways in this programme as Jane Root (Controller of BBC2) wants a female presenter and wants to make Clarissa Dickson-Wright the BBC's voice of the countryside'. I happen to like Clarissa but thought I was being treated rather shabbily. A few days later I mentioned the Equal Opportunities Commission to the producer. I also reminded him what he had said. 'I never said that', he responded. In other words I had developed a new medical condition – BBC telephonic hallucination.

The facts are that the BBC have got its terminology wrong. My attitude to 'One Man and His Dog' has not changed – it is the BBC's attitude to the programme that has changed and which I do not like. The Beeb unashamedly dumbed down the last 'Special' and by so doing managed to turn sheep dog trialling into a game show. It was demeaning for the shepherds, dog handlers and the viewers. Whoever heard of shepherds being put into coloured team shirts and being asked to jump around like village idiots? The programme was an insult to all those many thousands of people who enjoy untrivialised sheep dog trialling. If the BBC follows this path in other sports are we going to see footballers on Match of the Day playing in fancy dress? At this time, with shepherds and farmers facing desperate times, why can't they have their own programme and remember they were in crisis even before the arrival of foot and mouth. 24000 farmers and farm workers are being forced off the land each year. Farm incomes have dropped by 90% in five years and the average farm income is now half the national minimum wage.

The BBC's Nick Vaughan-Barratt says that the farce of coloured shirts and the forced jollity were to make sheep dog tri-alling more easy to understand. So who was his target audience – men from Mars? The new dumbed-down approach simply took the programme away from its natural audience and turned it into a piece of theme park countryside straight out of New Labour's long term rural vision. A few months ago I met the Director of Broadcasting, Mark Thompson, with Ms. Root. 'I can assure you Robin', he said, 'because of what you and the *Telegraph* did for *One Man and His Dog* you will not be blackballed'. If the sack isn't a rather extreme form of blackballing, I wonder what is?

The most worrying aspect of my demise must be the BBC's concerns for my 'other activities'. Two years ago if a Serbian broadcaster had been sacked by Serbian television for his opin-ions or activities the BBC would have rushed a film crew to him in order to fret about free speech and 'human rights'. Free speech and freedom of action for an excluded countryman is obviously of no concern.

So what are my other activities apart from farming? Publishing my book *The Hunting Gene* myself, when mainstream publishers would not touch it because of its political incorrectness, is one activity of which I am particularly proud. It has sold so well that I have had it reprinted twice. Jane Root turned it down as a series, although now it would be one of the most topical series on tele-vision. In my view the 'rejection' was political censorship. In addition, on publication 'The Gene' was completely ignored by all the BBC's national current affairs and 'country' programmes.

Three well known BBC contributors who support hunting asked not to be quoted in the book, for fear of losing their jobs; I now know why they were worried.

Oddly however, Root did manage to commission a major two part programme on animal rights, slanted heavily in favour of the animal rights lobby. It was very gentle concerning Labour's £1m donation and did not mention at all the generous payments made by animal rights organisations directly to other Labour politicians. It did not mention that the International Fund for Animal Welfare (UK) is a limited company and not a charity, nor that its founder is reported to have been paid a golden handshake of £1m on his retirement. It even failed to mention the tragedy that befell the Inuit people (eskimos) when they were unable to sell their seal skins from subsistence hunting after IFAW's misleading seal campaign.

My most important 'other activity' is as Chairman of the Countryside Restoration Trust. It takes up a considerable amount of my time, which I give quite freely, and from which I will not take a golden handshake. We are forging the way ahead for sensible, sustainable and responsible farming. We have been pioneering for farming, what the politicians are now urging at this tragic time. Even Tony Blair has used the word 'sustainable'; yet two years ago when we invited Tony Blair to see our project- he showed no interest whatsoever. Interestingly only on Thursday he claimed that the supermarkets have farming in an 'armlock'. In that case why hasn't he done something about it in four years? Instead he has stuffed his various task forces with supermarket directors, including six from Tesco. He gleefully accepted £12m from Tesco as sponsorship for the Dome and he appointed Labour donor Lord Christopher Haskins as Chairman of the Better Regulation Task Force – the organisation that should have stopped EU regulations closing down small slaughterhouses. In addition he has already had the domination of the supermarkets investigated by a committee. The report found little wrong and was printed in pure whitewash.

We have invited Nick Brown to our project three or four times – from his responses we may just as well have written to a moose.

We have even invited BBC's 'Countryfile', so far we have yet to receive an acknowledgement.

Less demanding, until the Euro referendum, is my role as Vice President of the Democracy Movement. My opposition to the EU stems from the unmitigated disaster known as the Common Agricultural Policy. It has led to the industrialisation of agriculture, which is almost certainly at the root of the present foot and mouth tragedy. In November I was proud to address an anti EU rally of 10,000 people in Trafalgar Square. It went unreported by the BBC, although a protest by 100 members of Black Britain in Whitehall was reported. The fact that the BBC is peopled by Europhiliacs could be part of my problem. Some time after my one and only appearance on 'Question Time' I was told that I would not be back because of my views on the EU. I expect that telephone call will also be attributed to BBC Telephonic Hallucination.

As a non-hunter, I also defend the right to hunt of those who choose to hunt. I am actually proud to defend hunting at this time; with the communities of Exmoor, the Lakes and rural Wales facing farming disaster, the recent anti-hunting Bill was an example of sheer political nastiness. I have been arrested once and if attacks on our rural way of life persist then Tony Blair should order several thousand new police vans in readiness for a huge wave of potential prisoners.

To me my sacking from "One Man and His Dog" shows exactly what the BBC thinks of the countryside and country people. It is political and social exclusion of the worst kind.

51

Stitched Up by the BBC

I know that I have just been sacked as presenter of "One Man and His Dog", but as if to rub salt into the wound, I, along with forty other innocent victims have just been stitched up by the BBC. We were invited to participate in the BBC's prime time 'Foot and Mouth Special'; each person thought that they had been asked to attend to make contributions to the programme. Apart from the animal rights representatives we were all wrong. Experts, farmers and butchers from all over Britain had been invited simply to provide human wallpaper for the BBC's studio set piece. This in turn was arranged to allow the Secretary of State for Agriculture, Nick Brown, to give almost a Party Political foot and mouth broadcast on behalf of the Labour Government. The rest of the programme was dedicated to turning foot and mouth into a cheap-jack game show complete with a viewer's poll at the end. So as thousands of animals burned; with many livestock farmers in despair and facing ruin, the BBC had turned, yet again, a serious country issue into trivial tinsel-town televised hype. Why serious and good broadcasters such as Nicky Campbell and Phillippa Forrester allowed themselves to be sucked into such a televised travesty is a mystery. Perhaps they were duped like the rest of us?

When the BBC contacted me to take part in the programme I told them honestly that if they simply wanted me as a member of the audience I would not attend. The battle for farming and the countryside is too serious and time is too short to allow for unessential ego-tripping around television studios. They assured me that I would be a real part of the programme. I said that I would not take part if there were more than thirty people in the

145

programme; they assured me that there were fewer than thirty studio guests – in fact there were forty two in London and a similar number scattered around other centres. I asked for an assurance that I would be asked specific questions – they gave that assurance. Apparently they gave similar assurances to the other guests; we were all misled by the BBC's culture of arrogance and deceit. To make it worse they even wanted us to spend the entire programme standing up 'as if we were at a market'. The rumblings of discontent caused an immediate rethink.

What took place was a television disgrace. Foot and mouth is a problem of farming and politics; the programme was turned into a food scare issue – which foot and mouth is not – and light entertainment. Rugby players and jockeys crying crocodile tears because their sports had been temporarily cancelled were featured before farmers. Television cameras and representatives of the BBC's light-weight 'Countryfile' programme dragged themselves and their cameras as close to diseased animals as possible, while telling everybody else to stay away. Busily scrubbing boots with disinfectant for effect and to justify their recklessness, they failed to say that one means of transporting the virus is actually in the human nose – next time, perhaps, presenter John Craven should be snorting disinfectant not scrubbing. There were sequences about e-coli and salmonella to music and an absurd piece about the electronic tagging of lambs, when one of Nick Brown's boasts is that he is reducing red tape and regulation.

By ignoring the real issues, it meant that Nick Brown was simply given a platform for self-justification. Without any doubt he is the worst Agricultural minister that I can remember; which is no mean feat when in competition with disasters such as Jack Cunningham and Douglas Hogg. His knowledge of farming and the countryside appears to be virtually nil and he seems to have become nothing but an errand boy flitting between Tony Blair and Brussels. With forty- two 'experts' present he was not asked one question directly by a member of the audience and Nicky Campbell protected him from actually becoming involved in a debate. He simply answered eight bland questions put to him by Campbell, allegedly lifted from e-mails. I have seen Brown protected like this before. On one occasion I was supposed to be on Channel 4 News with him. He only appeared on condition that he did not have to speak or debate directly with me.

The so-called 'studio debate' was equally absurd. I was the only person present involved in a charity with its own working farms. The Countryside Restoration Trust was established to show environmentally friendly farming in action. We have been preaching sustainable and responsible farming for seven years. Although both Brown and Blair have suddenly learnt the phrase 'sustainable farming', we have invited both to visit our farms and see our work; neither have shown the slightest interest or understanding. Others present were working farmers – one from Scotland, another from Shropshire, and a butcher who had had to hire extra labour for his shop to allow him to get to the studio. John Thorley of the National Sheep Association, Richard Burge of the Countryside Alliance and numerous others were all there. None were asked questions – instead the 'debate' simply gave free air time to various animal rights organisations. One vegetarian made my vegetarian niece embarrassed to be represented by such aggressive near hysteria.

The two key issues of foot and mouth and its spread were not discussed and Nick Brown was not confronted by them. The reason foot and mouth has spread so quickly is undoubtedly linked to the distance animals travel to slaughterhouses. This scandal is linked to the closure of local slaughter houses by idiotic and expensive EU regulations and also by the power of the supermarkets. They dictate which abattoirs their suppliers must use and they can be hundreds of miles from the farms on which the cattle, sheep and pigs are reared. EU regulations have scandalously closed down 800 slaughterhouses in the last ten years causing animal stress and the spread of disease. The BBC – the Brussels Broadcasting Service – controlled by Europhiliacs – obviously decided that the EU's idocy must not be on the agenda to avoid the ridiculing of both Brussels and Nick Brown.

The other issue, linked to the distances travelled by livestock to slaughter is the silence on the subject by the RSPCA. So why haven't programmes such as Watchdog and Countryfile highlighted this silence? The truth is that animals sold under the RSPCA's own label of 'Freedom Food' can travel hundreds of miles to slaughter making a mockery of the word 'freedom'. One West Sussex farmer was horrified when her animals were picked up for slaughter, courtesy of Freedom Food recently. The lorry was going on to Kent to pick up yet more animals and was then travelling to a huge slaughterhouse in Cornwall used by Tesco. Why hasn't the BBC exposed this – is its relationship with the RSPCA too cosy? Does it regard the RSPCA's 'Animal Hospital' and other anthropomorphic Bambi television as being more important that honesty?

As the programme finished and the lights dimmed, the studio manager had to muffle the microphone as the audience broke into almost open rebellion. People were angry at being both ignored and being expected to sit through such pure, unadulterated rubbish. Philippa Forrester appeared quite shaken at the anger. I have been sacked by the BBC for political incorrectness; I believe that more heads should roll for pure dumbed-down manipulation and political bias.

52

The Disaster That Need Not Have Happened

———

The foot and mouth epidemic currently sweeping through the country will be the last straw for many farmers. Despite the assertion made by Tony Blair almost exactly one year ago that there was no country crisis, the countryside is facing a disaster so large that we are in danger of losing our rural culture completely. The tragedy however is not that foot and mouth is here, but that the epidemic need not have happened. Our politicians and farming bureaucrats simply do not learn. The message from BSE was that industrialised, over intensive, 'efficient' farming contained many dangers and the time had come to change; nothing changed.

Now the scourge of foot and mouth has almost certainly come into the country through the importation of contaminated meat, either directly as meat from a country where foot and mouth is endemic, or in pig swill from the left-overs of airline food, again from a country where foot and mouth is endemic. Then, due to industrial farming the disease was introduced to intensively farmed pigs and then trailed across the country by transporting the animals unacceptable distances. A government that claims to be interested in animal welfare, particularly the welfare of 17000 foxes, has seen livestock carted hundreds of miles quite needlessly. Thirty-three and a half million pigs, cattle and sheep are involved in this absurdity every year and all the government does is close down yet more slaughterhouses; so making the situation worse. Even more unacceptably some cattle – herd animals – are mixed with animals from other herds during their journeys causing considerable distress.

The situation has been created by nonsensical European Regulations that have seen the closure of 800 slaughterhouses in the last ten years; this has meant the death of the local slaughterhouse. Once local environmental health officers could monitor slaughterhouses and the system worked well. Now vets have to be permanently on duty and slaughterhouses have been upgraded to ridiculous and expensive levels that go beyond simple hygiene and cleanliness. Farm livestock should not be faced with the stress of travelling long distances – they should be killed locally and if there is a need for long journeys it should be the carcasses that are transported. Obviously if there is a disease risk, of swine fever, or foot and mouth, then the threat is minimised when the animals travel just a few miles to slaughter. So why were animals being carted from Northumberland to Essex, and why are some animals trailed even longer distances every day of the year?

Part of the answer lies in the power of the supermarkets who now dominate the meat market. They want huge slaughterhouses with high throughputs for 'efficiency' and to reduce costs.

Interestingly the Essex outbreak of foot and mouth was not far from Tesco's Cheshunt headquarters; Tesco will not tell me whether any of the meat from the Essex slaughterhouse was destined for its shelves.

One of the largest slaughterhouses in the country, St. Meryn in Cornwall is used by Tesco. Neither Tesco nor the slaughterhouse will tell me the distances some of their animals travel; locals claim that some cattle arrive from as far away as Scotland.

The reason why the government takes no action is odd as Nick Brown, the Minister for Agriculture and Elliot Morley his underling claim to be passionate about animal welfare. Apparently fox hunting causes them immense distress, but trailing animals from one end of the country to the other worries them not at all. Perhaps that is why Nick Brown refers to 'product', not animals, when he talks about livestock farming.

The man in charge of overseeing 'regulation', including slaughter and transportation is Lord Christopher Haskins. He is Chairman of the Better Regulation Task Force. He is one of the biggest supporters of industrial farming in this country; he is a Europhile and he has ready access to both Tony Blair and Nick Brown. He is Chairman of Northern Foods and Express Dairies and he defends the regulations that are still closing down slaughterhouses. As 450 farmers and workers who are driven off the land each week, (24000 a year), and average farm incomes sink to half the national minimum wage, Lord Haskins is doing all right out of farming, thank you very much. Since 1992 he has given large donations to the Labour party and was made a peer in 1998. In that year he was paid £208,479 (plus share options that gained him £380,388) from Northern Foods. In the same year he received a £104,000 salary from Express Dairies.

Another disturbing feature in the whole scandal is the role of the RSPCA. Supposedly the RSPCA is concerned with animal welfare – again it is very worried about foxes; yet the RSPCA condones the transportation of farm animals over long distances and has been very quiet concerning the current crisis. The RSPCA even has its own food logo 'Freedom Food' which from its title implies animal welfare of the highest quality. Astonishingly,

'Freedom Food' does not have a mileage limit for animals transported in Britain; consequently animals trailed from
Northumberland to Essex, or Dumfries to Cornwall could be sold
as 'Freedom Food'. On talking to Ann Charlton of the RSPCA,
she claimed that she could not name any of the abattoirs, hauliers
and farms signed up to Freedom Food; she could not confirm that
some animals travelled from one end of the country to the other
and she could not say how much money the RSPCA receives
from its scheme. Normally it could be expected that the BBC
through the Today programme, Countryfile or Newsnight,
would be interested in the apparent contradictions involved in
Freedom Food, but there has been nothing on the airwaves.
Could this mean that the links between the RSPCA and the BBC
over Animal Hospital and other anthropomorphic media-mush
are too strong for proper investigative journalism?

The other scandal in a whole hotbed of scandal involves the
actual killing and burning of animals with foot and mouth. The
disease is not fatal; it does not threaten people and inoculation
can successfully overcome its spread. Prof. Donald Wilhelm of
Cambridge is involved in overseas development in both Africa
and Russia and has seen inoculation used extremely successfully.
Sadly MAFF seems to be stuck in a nineteen fifties time warp,
and this Labour Government is simply too agriculturally and
countryside illiterate to push them out of it.

The way forward according to Tim Lang, Professor of Food
Policy at Thames Valley University, is 'ecology friendly farming'.
The Countryside Restoration Trust of which I am Chairman has
been carrying this out in Cambridgeshire for several years. We
are producing good quality food; our livestock is killed locally
and our wildlife is flooding back. We have invited Nick Brown
and Tony Blair to see our form of farming, which we believe is
the way forward for the future, but they have shown absolutely
no interest whatsoever.

The current foot and mouth tragedy could have been avoided.
Those to blame are the politicians who are destroying responsi-
ble and sustainable farming – stand up the last government and
Tony Blair and his political and supermarket cronies.

53

Silent Summer

It is difficult to write about a tragedy, but in the circumstances I have no other option. With farming incomes and prospects at an all time low, foot and mouth was, and is the last straw for many farmers. At the time of writing this piece, we have escaped the dreaded symptoms in our sheep and cattle, but I can well imagine the sheer horror and despair when those dreaded blisters and lesions suddenly appear. During the course of the current epidemic I have had farming friends almost completely surrounded by the disease; life for them has become a time of tension and torment. I have had telephone calls too from complete strangers, they have had the disease and their voices have been full of despair, disbelief and anger. For them the summer fields are empty; there are no lambs, no calves and for some there seems to be no future and no hope. The year 2001 will linger long in the language of farming folklore; that is if there are any farmers left in thirty years time to remember and talk about times past.

To me, the scenes we have witnessed over recent weeks and months are unforgettable and unforgivable; a controllable disease, with little lasting impact on the animals it affects, in a modern, First World country, has been regarded a cruel scourge and treated in a way that can only be described as medieval. Thousands upon thousands of good, healthy animals have been massacred and burnt as if part of some primitive Satanic ritual. Funeral pyres have been seen smouldering for days; piles of uncovered bodies have been left at roadsides and human feelings have been totally disregarded as the politicians have recited their favourite, empty and meaningless mantras, 'the slaughter policy must continue' and 'we have the outbreak under control'.

In the middle of all the mindless Ministry induced claptrap and mayhem I received a telephone call from a friend who lives in Kenya. 'What is going on in England Robin?' he asked, 'Have the politicians lost the plot? I worked on a farm in Kenya in the 'Fifties which developed foot and mouth. The old colonial service vets came out and said 'Leave it and it will quickly be over'. Within a month it had swept through the entire herd and we only lost two animals. Most just suffered minor discomfort and the biggest problem was when a cow with a calf went dry and had no milk. Foot and mouth may be a highly contagious disease, but it is not a serious problem'.

Worse was to follow. It quickly became clear that if the Ministry had invested just a fraction of the money they spent on fighting the disease, and paying compensation, on development and research into combating foot and mouth, they would have been able to develop an effective vaccination without causing any long term economic damage. Sadly that is the crux of the whole foot and mouth tragedy; financial considerations have been given a higher priority than farmer welfare and animal welfare. A country in which foot and mouth disease is present can, in normal circumstances, not export meat or animals to other countries. One of the main exceptions to this rule is, of course Britain; as we have various beef importing agreements with countries where foot and mouth disease is endemic, such as South Africa, Botswana and even Zimbabwe. Consequently the export market was considered to be a higher priority than morality.

I had another telephone call too, which put the activities of the politicians (of all parties) and officials into their true perspective. Dr. Tim Coulson is a wildlife biologist working at Cambridge University; he said 'It is a ridiculous situation that we have the capability to inoculate animals and protect them from disease but are unable to do so for purely economic and political reasons. Especially as the technology exists that should allow the development of a vaccine that would allow us to distinguish between diseased and inoculated animals'. The use of such a vaccine in animals surrounding an outbreak would quickly contain that

153

outbreak and if used in Devon, Cumbria, Northumberland and Essex would have contained this outbreak. Then, once the disease had been stopped in its tracks, blood tests could be taken and it would be possible to detect which animals carried antibodies from the vaccine and which were carriers of the actual disease. With the few carriers killed, the herds would again be disease free and within a year meat and animals could again be exported; believe it or not, the solution to foot and mouth disease really is as simple as that.

Again, the scaremongerers are not satisfied with such simplicity. They claim that in such circumstances foot and mouth disease would become endemic in Britain. This too, is totally wrong. Over the years, due to the arrival of travellers and animals from abroad, Britain has suffered from both foot and mouth disease and rabies. The diseases have swept through the country and then died out naturally, simply because conditions in this country do not favour either of them. Consequently, the short term use of vaccination will not suddenly cause the disease to become 'endemic'.

Since the last outbreak of foot and mouth disease in 1967 there has been another significant development which makes the policy of culling a complete nonsense. There are now more wild deer in Britain than there have been for several hundred years. In Cumbria and Devon there are red deer and roe, and throughout the country there are growing populations of red, roe and fallow. In addition, the small muntjac deer is doing a wonderful job of colonising and there are also pockets of sika and Chinese water deer. With foot and mouth disease rampant it would be impossible to mount an effective cull against deer, particularly a cull against muntjac.

Despite the self-congratulation of some politicians and officials, the way in which the foot and mouth outbreak has been handled has been nothing short of scandalous. It can only be hoped that before the next outbreak, important lessons will have been learnt and that a proper and up-to-date vaccine will have been developed. Farmers, livestock and the whole countryside deserve nothing less.

54

Assassinated Character

———

Oh dear, I am in great trouble. I have had a number of telephone calls asking me how Corset is; whether she has gone back to the Kennels of the Cambridgeshire Hunt, or even, whether she has been run over by a bus? I have to say that Corset is fit and well; in fact from the evidence of my nose and ears she is positively booming. The delay in passing on her adventures has simply and tragically been caused by foot and mouth disease. Although the BBC have sacked me since the arrival of the current epidemic, much of the media, the BBC included, have wanted to know what is going on, and the phone never stops ringing.

Poor Corset has been devastated by events – first my sacking, then foot and mouth and then the cancellation of the March. To top it all she has come on heat again, three months before she was due; thank goodness Jonah at the farmhouse is two stones lighter than he once was and so Corset is in no conjugal danger.

As if all this was not enough, Corset has been very upset by two journalists. One of indeterminate sex – from its name at least – called Francis Spleen, and the other a woman from that little read newspaper, *The Independent*. For some unknown reason they seem not to like country people and me in particular and so I have been 'stitched-up' twice in the Press recently. Fortunately, nearly all the 'facts' have been fiction, which means that if sections of the politically correct media have to resort to fantasy, then the battle to get the voice of the countryside heard, must be being won.

The *Independent* woman was a remarkable creature from Inner M25 land – Lewisham; she was Lewisham Lady as opposed to Essex girl. On seeing Corset she drew back in horror – an animal!

155

Corset drew back too as the creature in front of her was almost unrecognisable from the normal people who visit my cottage – sorry, semi-detached kennel. Lewisham Lady was carrying bags, wearing a long coat and once off the pavement she staggered. She would have made an excellent resident of Fawlty Towers. 'What is the dog?' she squeaked. 'A foxhound', I replied. Her eyes rolled and I thought she was going to swoon. That put me in a panic – I certainly had no intention of giving her the kiss of life – neither would I allow Corset such a daunting task. Fortunately she recovered just as I was searching for the tractor tyre pump. Recovery was a great shame: 'I thought you couldn't keep fox-hounds as pets?' she asked with a triumphant sneer.

'You can't', I responded and gave her a tour of the house; the damaged doors when Corset was shut in and I was out; the foot-prints on the spare bed; the pig's ear in the armchair and the hairs on every square inch of carpet – yes, Corset is moulting, like a female William Hague. Corset was not impressed by all this per-ceived criticism and went off for a drink from the lavatory.

'As she is so obviously a pet, would you like her to sit on your lap when she comes down' I asked quite innocently, 'she is only a puppy' (albeit a seventy pound one). Lewisham Lady declined. She conducted the interview, uneasily accepting Corset at her feet, and visibly wincing when I gave her answers she clearly did not want to hear. 'You are here just to stitch me up', I told her. She muttered something about journalism and being interested in my life and attitudes. Corset was not impressed.

As the journalist finished and left again for Inner M25 land, her map book must have fallen out of her coat pocket – a Polyester leopard skin coat. Corset and I live just three and a half miles from Cambridge station, yet Lewisham Lady had had to use a map – in a taxi! Never mind, one of the pages came in very handy to clean the lipstick off her coffee mug.

A few days later a friend bought a copy of the *Independent*. They had used the most unflattering photograph of me ever taken and plastered it all over the front page. Then I saw the greatest journalistic sin that there has ever been – Lewisham Lady had insulted Corset. 'Walking up the front garden of Robin

Page's Cambridgeshire cottage, the first thing to strike you is the slobbery nose of his yobbish foxhound, Corset, somewhere around crutch level'. I am sorry, in my view where Corset's nose happens to be says more about the personal hygiene of any visitors, than the degree of slobberyness of her nose. In addition of course, how on earth could anybody call the best looking lady foxhound in Britain, yobbish? A female yob? Perhaps Lewisham Lady can't tell the difference between a dog and a lady dog, (I can't bring myself to call Corset a bitch).

Oh well, I've learnt my lesson; I will never allow another journalist into my house unless they come from some highly respected magazine or newspaper such as *Horse and Hound*, *Home and Garden*, or the *Sunday Sport*.

55

Lakeland Tragedy

―――

As the funeral pyres of Cumbria burn and smoulder, the whole countryside is swathed in a haze of smoke. It is a haunting, tragic scene as hill farmers and shepherds, already caught up in a financial and social crisis, see that crisis turn into a disease induced disaster. Lives are being shattered and a whole culture is being threatened. The tragedy travels beyond the people and the communities directly affected and extends to the farm animals – both healthy and infected – that are being sentenced to death.

To see bodies heaped up by the roadside, and smell the stench, gives a strange medieval aspect to 'Britain in the 21st century'. To me, the mass slaughter is a crime, ordered by urban, out of touch politicians and carried out with the connivance of a moribund government department and a compliant, fawning union.

Where fires have ceased to smoke the fields are quiet. Around the emptiness there is fear, for gradually the silence is spreading.

It has crept from the Solway to the rolling meadows around Wigton and now it is edging into the valleys of the Lakes themselves. There, as smiling politicians say 'The countryside is open for business', farmers fearing the worst are living in barricaded isolation.

The Lake District is a beautiful place; an island of rural peace and tranquillity in an over-populated and urban land. There are farms, fields and fells where communities still live on and from the land. Despite their hard lives the people are warm and welcoming. When I took part in my first 'One Man and His Dog' series, before the programme had been dumbed down into inner-M25 absurdity, the locals of Buttermere made me very welcome. The competition was filmed on the farm of Willie Richardson, whose family has been farming around the edge of that wild, beautiful lake for three generations. It was there that I saw at close quarters for the first time that unique sheep of the Lakeland fells, the Herdwick.

The Herdwick must be one of the most attractive breeds of sheep in the world. It looks almost like a fleecy teddy bear with cloven hooves. It is hardy; it is intelligent – for a sheep – and it does extremely well in the harsh, cold and wet conditions of the Lake District. Where the breed originated from is unknown. Stories suggest that it has been part of the local landscape for hundreds of years.

One tale suggests that a foundering Spanish galleon, seeking escape, finally went down off the Cumbrian coast. The sheep on board, once destined for the mariners' dinner plate, swam ashore to freedom and found the area very much to their liking. They have been there ever since. A more likely story claims that Scandinavian raiders brought it with them and for the Herdwick it was a case of home from home. Confirmation of the Viking connection comes from the Thirteenth Century where mention is made of the Herdwick. In Norse the name is derived from two words 'wick' which means place and herd – the place of the herd.

However the Herdwick arrived in Britain, it has become an established part of the Lake District's farming pattern and it was both loved and promoted by Beatrix Potter. Sadly, part of that same farming pattern now threatens the sheep. Before foot and mouth, the Herdwick was not even a 'rare breed'. After foot and mouth it looks as if it will be an endangered species.

For years most of the sheep from the fells, the hogs (hoggs, hoggerels or hoggets) – a male or female sheep between being weaned and shorn for the first time – the shearlings – a young sheep between its first and second shearing – as well as the rams, have gone down to the low, rich grazing meadows of the Solway Plain and the Eden valley for the winter. Willie's grandfather originally walked them along old drove roads, showing that the current hysteria claiming that winter sheep movements are new, are urban, political myths. Local railways were also used for the seasonal movement of sheep, and Willie's animals are now taken by lorry.

This traditional movement meant that when foot and mouth struck in the Solway and the Eden valley, most of the Lake District's Herdwicks were away from the hills and were in what has become the heart of the culling zone. More seriously, much of the Lake District is now classified as an 'Environmentally Sensitive Area', and the strict MAFF rules require larger numbers being removed from the winter fells than in the past. Tragically, the time between writing this article and seeing it in print, will be the time that Willie Richardson loses 1100 of his 1700 sheep. It is a personal loss for which money can provide no adequate compensation. Vaccination could have saved valuable breeding stock, but MAFF (the Ministry Against Farmers and Farming), and the NFU (No Flipping Use) have moved sluggishly both mentally and physically and have opposed inoculation. Their indecision and ill-informed prevarication will mean that most of the young Herdwick breeding stock of the Lakes will die. Before foot and mouth there were 75,000 Herdwick ewes in the Lakes. Already up to 20% have been culled and it is feared that if the disease continues on its current course the number of casualties could be almost 100%, leaving a varied stock of some 3000 largely ornamental Herdwicks in various parts of the country.

Even those pregnant ewes still in the Fells, following their traditional seasonal pattern, and due to lamb at the end of April, are not safe. Each day the disease moves nearer and the threat becomes greater. Worse still, at this time the ewes are usually moved off the hills for better grazing, to ensure strong healthy lambs. Now, because of foot and mouth restrictions they cannot be moved and soon they will be lambing without good food and in harsh conditions– mortality of both lambs and ewes will be high. The Herdwick is important for other reasons. The landscape of the Lakes is a grazed landscape, made and renewed annually by the native sheep. In addition the Herdwick has a very special feature, and again its Norse name describes the characteristic. The ewes become established on certain fells, their home range, and after lambing in the valley, the females take their lambs back onto those home fells and the new lambs learn from their mothers where they are supposed to be. In the dialect of the Lakes they become 'heafed' or hefted sheep and less likely to wander off their part of the fells.

If the Herdwick disappears from the Lakes it will be a calamity, and there are numerous farmers facing the same heartbreak as Willie Richardson. Tragically unless realistic action is taken quickly, extinction will spread from the sheep to the farms and farmers themselves. I suspect that is what some of the Government's farming advisers and politicians, actually want.

56

A Night of Passion

For a disease that has been 'under control' since the very first day of the very first outbreak, foot and mouth has lasted a very long time. If foot and mouth really was under control, I wonder how many animals would have been slaughtered and lives ruined if it had been 'out of control'; perhaps I had better ask MAFF's performing ventriloquist's dummy, Nick Brown. Well, there's a thought, having Nick Brown sit on your lap while he mouths his master's mantra: 'It's under control; it's under control'. Sadly his imagination has been wildly out of control and I think that I would rather have a massive dose of foot and mouth than have that squat-featured Geordie dumpling sit on my lap.

I mention foot and mouth as it seems such a long time ago since the disease struck. I remember the outbreak very well as it occurred just as I returned from a brief trip away with a very beautiful girl. Yes, I took Corset on holiday to the seaside; she is a lucky bitch. How many other foxhounds in the country can boast of having had a hot water bottle on very cold nights and a holiday by the sea? I did not pack a bucket and spade but I had a huge supply of dog leads and whistles. I took binoculars too as I had visions of seeing the white tip of her tail disappearing from the end of Blakeney Point before I had even got second wind. I took a world record number of Bonios and chews as well, in case she responded better to straightforward bribes instead of words of command.

My problem was that at the mention of a few days away, all my usual hound-minders suddenly had full diaries, or developed headaches. One in total panic even started decorating his bed-room; something his wife had never seen before in twenty-five years of marriage. So there was only one thing for it; the most beautiful hound in Britain would have to visit Norfolk with me.

Stiffkey is a wonderful little village. Clever people still argue in the national press over its long departed vicar. If a vicar accused of having friendly relationships with young ladies decides to prove his innocence or guilt by putting his head in a lion's mouth, and the lion decides to bite – then I would have thought that the verdict was quite clear cut. But the argument still rages; as does the controversy about Henry Williamson, author of *Tarka the Otter*, who spent the Second World War farming at Stiffkey. Then, many people regarded him as a 'Fascist scoundrel' because of his views on Europe. Today those same views would have placed him as middle of the road New Labour. At least Henry Williamson's views on hunting, farming and the countryside had nothing in common with New Labour.

Corset loved her new kennel – an old fisherman's hut, now a small bungalow, within crawling distance of the Red Lion. It is a wonderful pub selling Norfolk's own perfect amber nectar, Woodeford's Wherry Ale; it also allows dogs to share the comfort of the three open fires. Whether the landlord would allow the ventriloquist's dummy to sit on anybody's lap in the public bar has yet to be tested. The hound loved the salt marshes and the sea too. My old lurcher, Bramble, enjoyed the salt marshes at Stiffkey. He would run in huge circles leaping over the gullies and creeks with grace and agility. Corset was equally moved by the wide-open spaces, without the grace or agility. By the time she had finished she resembled a mud-plough, made worse by rolling in what appeared to be a dead haddock. Her appearance and smell were both absolutely disgusting – like visiting the Cabinet Office during a discussion on political donations. Isn't it odd, anti-hunting Nick Brown's policies have notched up millions of dead animals. Anti-hunting Elliot Morley's policies have lead to the dumping of millions of dead haddock; I wonder if they are paid on a bonus scheme?

As the sun set I was almost at the water's edge. I froze in horror. Suddenly Corset's nose went down and her tail went up and she was off into the gloom. What she was hunting I have no idea; a limpet, one of the thousands of wintering geese or even, possibly, one of Mr. Morley's haddock? The wild geese are spectacular in a Norfolk winter. At a Press Conference recently I asked that well known goose expert, Nick Brown, if geese were helping to spread foot and mouth around the Solway. 'No' he said simply. The next day the Norwegian government advised its farmers to keep their cattle in until migrating geese from Britain had passed through, thus avoiding any risk of goose carried foot and mouth. To this day I'm sure the ventriloquist's dummy thought I was talking about farmyard geese.

Eventually, in almost total darkness, with the tide rushing in, the errant hound returned still covered in Norfolk slime, having had a wonderful time. I was exhausted and hoarse. Corset gleefully greeted a young lady taking an evening walk by placing two huge mud spattered paw prints in the middle of her chest.

She smiled and patted the haddock scented canine; I've never had that sort of response from such a greeting.

That night I had a major worry. Corset had never slept in a house before and the big question was, would her digestive system last the night. She's a very regular dog; she appears to answer the call of nature about 5am, but unfortunately she does not get up until eight. In case of emergency activity in the living room, I slept with the bedroom door open. Tired, warm, comfortable and Wherry happy I fell asleep. It was a wonderful dream, suddenly my luck had changed. A beautiful young lady jumped on me; the duvet was pulled off, I was locked in a passionate embrace; her hot breath was on my cheeks, her tongue was on my lips, and then I smelt that unmistakable smell – very, very old haddock. Yes, Corset was on top of me and evicting me from my bed. Every night after that, sleep turned into nightmare at about 1.30am, but at least *she* was warm and comfortable.

As usual it was a wonderful stay, but sadly, by the time I got home the bed stealing and the mud sliding of the haddock hunter meant that I was in urgent need of a holiday.

57

More Victim Support

———

I am sitting here pen in one hand and tissue in the other; I am not crying with laughter or sorrow – I have a streaming cold – and Corset is sitting looking at me, wondering what has crawled into my lungs to make so much noise. Dogs do not seem to have much knowledge of the human body and when I relax in my armchair she tries to sit on my chest; it is not much fun having a seventy-pound foxhound (puppy) crushing your bronchials. At on point in the fight to get her off, she was even sitting on my head barking; who says that foxhounds can be 'homed'?

At that point I was actually relieved to have my cold, for when Corset returns to me, after breaks at the Cambridgeshire Hunt Kennels, her diet changes; this means that as Bonios meet yesterday's dead cow – mid-way between her mouth and her tail – spectacular internal and external combustion takes place. Fortunately on this occasion my congestion kept me blissfully unaware of the full impact of her efforts to increase global warming.

I think my cold is due to a sudden dose of Pennine cooling. After my recent visit to see the threatened Herdwick sheep of Cumbria I took every precaution to prevent spreading foot and mouth myself. This meant that on my return journey I stopped in a small wood just off the A66. There I took off every stitch of clothing, including my wellington boots and put them into a tightly tied dustbin bag. I was not a pretty sight – a white shivering tub of lard, standing totally exposed in a sunlit glade. I suppose that if I had thought quickly enough I could have charged an entrance fee and become one of Mr. Blair's famous 'countryside attractions'. My state of nudity lasted only as long as it takes to put on another set of carefully tailored clothes, followed by a drenching of the nostrils with Glycerine of Thymol. Yes, forget most of what you have heard concerning the foot and mouth virus – one of its favoured refuges is the human nostril. With his quivering nasal passages, this makes our Prime Minister one of the most dangerous and likely carriers.

On arrival home the bag of discarded clothes was shut in a wardrobe for a fortnight – with the well used wellington boots apparently killing the woodworm. To make doubly sure of no disease I broke my rule of only bathing on the longest day and the shortest day by having a long, hot shower. Corset hates the downstairs ablutions and will still only drink from the upstairs lavatory.

Feeling beautifully clean and smelling fragrant – a local Cambridgeshire characteristic, I decided to do some farm work; after all I am no longer the 'ol boy', I am now the farmer, as my brother has retired. I loaded the horse trailer with wire and posts and fought with Corset for ten minutes to get her off the Fourtrak's driver's seat. On the way to the soggy field Corset again managed to sit on my head – at thirty miles an hour; things will have to change as this could lead to the police arresting me again; they have to have some successes.

Thanks to Cambridgeshire County Council my burst of activity failed to last long. One of their overflowing drains had turned the field entrance into a bog, where the trailer became totally stuck. To get a better view Corset backed into the electric fence and was last seen heading north crying like a baby – another countryside visitor attraction?

By unhitching the trailer I managed to escape in the knowledge that the trailer was safe. If it was stuck, any didecoy trying to steal it would also become stuck. Alas, in a way, I had spoken too soon, for on arriving back at the farmyard, didecoys had struck there. All my pink diesel had either been stolen or was flowing into the ditch.

I phoned 999. The police emergency service could not have been less interested – didecoy crime in Cambridgeshire is out of control – and gave me another number. On that, a new police constable showed a similar lack of interest. I told him of my concern at the diesel getting into the ditch and flowing on into the brook 'so can you give me the emergency number for the Environment Agency please?'

The answer I received was the most astonishing I have ever received – even from the Cambridgeshire Constabulary: 'I don't know anything about that sir, why don't you look in Yellow Pages'. I never did see a policeman or anybody from the Environment Agency, although I did get the usual letter from Victim Support – I'll soon be able to paper my living room walls with them.

Never mind, the Cambridgeshire police have just informed all villages that twenty police officers have been removed from normal duties to fight homophobic and racist crime. They did say neither is a problem at the moment in rural Cambridgeshire, but they want to be prepared. That makes me feel a lot better; so the Cambridgeshire Constabulary is winning the battle against non-existent crime; I wonder when they will take an interest in the real thing.

58

The Curse of the Haddock

What is the difference between a Blair Babe and a Haddock? One is smooth, oily with a great big mouth and huge bulging eyes and the other is a fish.

I start with this piece of useful political information because the Curse of the Haddock has struck, or should it be the Curse of Elliot Morley? Elliot Morley you will remember is that wonderful animal welfare loving MP who is anti-foxhunting. Why anybody from Scunthorpe should be worried about an activity that does not take place in Scunthorpe is another matter entirely, although of course as Elliot Morley admits himself, he has received money from an anti-hunting organisation in the past. As you would expect from a member of a political party that keenly supported the idea of 'Freedom of Information' when in opposition, Elliot Morley will not say how much he has received. It seems to be a case of Freedom of Information for everybody else – oh what a surprise.

Well, Elliot Morley 'Mr. Humanitarian' from Scunthorpe, former Council Member of the RSPB happens to be our Fisheries Minister, who is currently seeing millions of young haddock tipped back into the sea by British fishermen. They have caught the haddock accidentally and as they have no quotas for haddock, they are having to tip millions of dead haddock back into the sea. This is known as 'fish conservation' as far as the Common Fisheries Policy is concerned. What I want to know is why a picture of a young haddock has not appeared on every newspaper front page in Britain, like Phoenix the calf, leading to an instant reprieve from the great and good Tony Blair. Think of all those poor, traumatised mother haddock, who just need to see

166

their children again. Part of the trouble is that many young female Labour MP's, the Blair Babes, do actually look as if they are related to haddock. On the face of it too, I suppose, Cherie Blair could even be a genetically modified haddock; who can tell?

I mention all this because the other day, well after her famous haddock hunt in Norfolk, Corset found a dead fish. It was not a haddock, but a pike, but the effect was just the same and I wonder if it had been put there by Elliot Morley? The cattle had just been turned out to pasture. It had rained solidly for two days and the cattle had been shut up indoors again. I had gone with the dogs to check the state of the grazing and quickly went to where I should have had a few meadow fritillary wildflowers growing. It was Jonah who spotted the pike first, presumably with his nose. The poor fish had been swimming on the meadow when the floods were up, but had been marooned when the floods had gone down, and so here it was doing its dead haddock impersonation.

I knew I was in trouble when Jonah started rolling with his legs in the air; he was in a state of nasal ecstasy. Then Corset bounded over to oust him, she had 'Cor, I think I will have a bit of that' written all over her face. I arrived at the dead fish just as Corset was in the middle of her second roll. The stench was absolutely disgusting, just like the Cabinet Room on the day they decided to save Phoenix the calf.

I chased Corset off; alas I was too late. In quite simple mathematical terms her smell was about ten times worse than her haddock rolling efforts in Norfolk. I picked up the evil smelling fish determined to throw it into the brook and out of harm's way; suddenly it was wrenched out of my hand and Corset, fish in mouth was making off into the distance. She had crept up behind me and simply stolen the decaying pike. The louder I shouted and the faster I ran, the further Corset's relaxed lopes took her away from me.

Once at a safe distance, biologists would call it the 'flight distance', Corset dropped the fish. She stepped back, looked at it and then dived in as if she was bungy jumping on the evil smelling carcass. She rolled, she rocked, her legs were in the air, at one time she looked as if she was even doing a head stand on the rotting heap of scales. By the time she would let me near, I did not want to get anywhere near her. She was just disgusting: I did manage to retrieve the fish but it was too late. I threw it into the brook happy that I would never see it again; although it took screams at parade ground decibel level to stop the dogs retrieving it. The smell in the back of the car, with both dogs wagging their tails to get complete air circulation was a nasal nightmare, the likes of which I have never experienced before and never want to experience again.

The only good thing about the incident was that I have just had a dog guard fitted to my Fourtrak. As a result both dogs were safely in the back of the car, and it meant that I did not have Corset trying to sit on my lap, attempting to cover me with her new overall body scent. Jonah, liking water as he does was not a problem; he was soaped and scrubbed and was soon almost tolerable. Corset hates water and she would have none of it. 'Here', 'Sit', 'Steady', 'Corset you miserable swine, will you come here and do as you are told' were words that had all suddenly lost their meaning.

Even now, several days later, she carries a slightly fishy odour and on returning to the brook meadows both dogs sprinted to the exact spot where I had thrown the disgusting fish back into the water. Thank goodness it had disappeared. If it really was the Curse of Elliot Morley then I will never say anything bad about the man again, unless of course, he deserves it.